Hadar Lubin, MD
David Read Johnson, PhD

Trauma-Centered Group Psychotherapy for Women
A Clinician's Manual

Pre-publication
REVIEW

"This intelligent book explains how and why a therapist can provide a powerful group experience to traumatized women. In this clear and concise guide for clinicians, the authors convey their sixteen-week method for weekly outpatient small-group treatment, including theory, case discussion, and evidence of impact. Any therapist contemplating a group approach for trauma survivors would be remiss to not read this book. Clinicians treating individuals will pick up valuable insights about combining education with re-experiencing, about managing social isolation, and about instilling optimism in ways that work. This is an encouraging book for every trauma therapist."

Frank M. Ochberg, MD,
Former Associate Director, NIMH,
Clinical Professor of Psychiatry,
Michigan State University; Recipient,
Lifetime Achievement Award, ISTSS

Trauma-Centered Group Psychotherapy for Women
A Clinician's Manual

The Haworth Press®
Titles of Related Interest

Trauma-Centered Group Psychotherapy for Women
A Clinician's Manual

Hadar Lubin, MD
David Read Johnson, PhD

The Haworth Press
Taylor & Francis Group
New York and London

For more information on this book or to order, visit
http://www.haworthpress.com/store/product.asp?sku=6097

or call 1-800-HAWORTH (800-429-6784) in the United States and Canada
or (607) 722-5857 outside the United States and Canada

or contact orders@HaworthPress.com

The Haworth Press, Taylor & Francis Group, 270 Madison Avenue, New York, NY 10016.

PUBLISHER'S NOTE
The development, preparation, and publication of this work has been undertaken with great care. However, the Publisher, employees, editors, and agents of The Haworth Press are not responsible for any errors contained herein or for consequences that may ensue from use of materials or information contained in this work. The Haworth Press is committed to the dissemination of ideas and information according to the highest standards of intellectual freedom and the free exchange of ideas. Statements made and opinions expressed in this publication do not necessarily reflect the views of the Publisher, Directors, management, or staff of The Haworth Press, Inc., or an endorsement by them.

Identities and circumstances of individuals discussed in this book have been changed to protect confidentiality.

Cover design by Jennifer Gaska.

Library of Congress Cataloging-in-Publication Data

Trauma-centered group psychotherapy for women : a clinician's manual / Hadar Lubin, David Read Johnson, editors.
  p. ; cm.
Includes bibliographical references.
ISBN 978-0-7890-3682-7 (hard : alk. paper)
ISBN 978-0-7890-3683-4 (soft : alk. paper)
  1. Post-traumatic stress disorder—Treatment. 2. Group psychotherapy. 3. Women—Mental health. I. Lubin, Hadar. II. Johnson, David Read.
  [DNLM: 1. Stress Disorders, Post-Traumatic—therapy. 2. Psychotherapy, Group—methods. 3. Women's Health. WM 170 T77733 2007]
RC552.P67T7475 2007
616.85'21—dc22
                                                        2007034361

About the Authors

Hadar Lubin, MD, is a board certified psychiatrist, Assistant Clinical Professor in the Department of Psychiatry at Yale University School of Medicine, and Co-Director of the Post Traumatic Stress Center in New Haven, Connecticut. Dr. Lubin has worked for many years with clients who have had a wide range of trauma exposure and clinical manifestations, both in inpatient and outpatient settings. She has extensive experience in psychotherapy with trauma-centered perspectives and in the pharmacological management of trauma-related disorders. In 1994, she founded the Women's Trauma Program at Yale and has since developed other specialized treatments for trauma survivors. Dr. Lubin has published extensively and conducts research in PTSD.

David Read Johnson, PhD, is a licensed clinical psychologist, Associate Clinical Professor in the Department of Psychiatry at Yale University School of Medicine, and the Co-Director of the Post Traumatic Stress Center. Dr. Johnson was formerly the Unit Chief of the Specialized Inpatient PTSD unit at the National Center for PTSD, VA Medical Center in West Haven, Connecticut. His area of expertise is in the treatment of psychological trauma and he has developed and researched a number of treatment models for individual, group, couples, and family therapy, both with veterans and the general population.

CONTENTS

Foreword

"Social healing for social injury."

(Sandra Bloom, 1997)

As a long-time proponent of the viewpoint espoused in this quote regarding healing from psychological trauma, it is a pleasure to write the Foreword for this book on an innovative model of group psychotherapy for women trauma survivors. The Trauma-Centered Group Psychotherapy model developed by Hadar Lubin and David R. Johnson and described in this book is founded on this same perspective: the group setting provides a unique context and important benefits in sustaining women as they heal from the effects of psychological trauma. The support of others has been found to be essential to the healing process, whatever the type of trauma. This is especially the case when the trauma was interpersonal and committed intentionally by someone known to the victim, an unfortunate reality for many women who are more likely to know their assailant as family member or friend than are male victims who are more likely to be assaulted by strangers. The resulting psychological trauma has personal and interpersonal spin-offs that can be debilitating and can impact the victim over the course of her entire life. I suggest that the same is true for male victims (possibly from different trauma dynamics) and that a modification of this model would be quite therapeutic for them as well.

Group involvement is meaningful for many reasons, among them a decrease in the sense of isolation as well as in shame and stigmatization associated with trauma that comes from being with others who had similar experiences. Furthermore, group involvement provides the opportunity to support others while being supported by them, no small feat with individuals who are mistrustful and expect to be hurt by others rather than assisted by them. The unique benefit of the group setting is that it provides a context or "holding environment" within which to do healing work while simultaneously functioning as a catalyst to the work.

The Trauma-Centered Group Psychotherapy model is theoretically derived and based on a trauma-informed developmental approach yet it is very integrative of a variety of treatment perspectives and models (experiential, cognitive-behavioral, trauma-referenced, psychodynamic, systems, among others). Quite significantly, in this age of evidence-based practice, it was developed and adapted based upon other available group treatment models, from qualitative outcome data gathered from all participants along with the observations and experience of the co-leaders (it has now been offered thirty times over the span of twelve years), and from the increasingly available empirical outcome data on group and individual treatments for trauma survivors.

Although TCGP has a resemblance to other group models, it has a number of unique features. It was deliberately developed for individuals with heterogeneous rather than homogeneous trauma experiences in order to support processing of *the experience* of the trauma rather than the specific *type* of trauma. It has been effectively offered to individuals who were multiply as well as singly traumatized, and has proven therapeutic to those with a wide range of posttraumatic adaptations and disorders, including those who suffer from chronic psychiatric illness. In keeping with the research supporting exposure as a treatment of choice for the traumatized, it promotes the disclosure of the traumatic experience right from the start of the group; however, in keeping with the literature on the need for stability and containment before trauma processing, it has a unique session sequence that is highly structured. Each session begins and ends with a didactic presentation while the middle of each involves processing of group dynamics and the impact of the traumatic material. The overall program is relatively short-term, offered in ninety-minute sessions over the course of sixteen weeks.

Drs. Lubin and Johnson's three-stage developmental model of trauma aftereffects is state-of-the-art and has been used creatively as the foundation for this group treatment. At its core, a developmental model is used from which to understand the aftereffects of trauma both in the short-term and over the lifespan. Trauma, at any point in the life cycle but especially when it occurs in childhood, interferes with the normal developmental tasks of accommodation and assimilation, thus creating impairment in the individual's capacity for differentiation. This impaired capacity, in turn, results in primary effects that, without effective intervention, develop into secondary effects, and finally tertiary effects. Primary effects involve sensory processing deficits, affect dysregulation, faulty cognitions/schemas about self and others, and maladaptive interpersonal relations. Secondary adaptations involve the development of defenses and other coping methods (i.e., projection, denial, dissociation, risk-taking, substance abuse, self-injury), used to avoid the disturbing trauma-related experiences and feelings. Tertiary effects involve disruptions in the individual's systems of meaning, resulting in feelings of hopelessness, despair, chronic mistrust, and demoralization and interfering with the ability to mourn losses associated with the trauma.

This treatment model systematically addresses these three levels across the sequence of the treatment, with the first phase of five weeks devoted to explaining and processing primary effects, the second of six weeks to the secondary coping effects, and the third of five weeks to the tertiary systems of meaning. Each session is devoted to a specific topic and involves an opening and wrap-up lecture presented by the co-leaders followed by discussion and processing in the midsection of the session. At the end of the entire program, members have a graduation or witnessing ceremony to which they invite significant others in their lives to whom they disclose the trauma and its impact. This step, another innovation of this treatment model, is designed to bring the trauma to the larger community and for its members to witness it and assist victims in the resolution of its consequences. Group members break their silence by disclosing and symbolically and practically "turning over" their trauma to caring family members and friends in the community. Through this process, they are no longer hidden and isolated and the stigmatization is resolved.

Readers will find this book well-written and extremely accessible as a treatment manual. For professionals who intend to use this model, they will find it ready-to-use, complete with detailed instructions for teaching the content, with handouts that can be replicated, and with case examples and metaphors that are highly explanatory. The session topics and content are presented in very understandable terms. Complicated material is communicated clearly and succinctly, making it highly accessible for the participants.

Since this is a content-focused and change-oriented experiential treatment model, a specific goal is for participants to change long-standing schemas and behavioral/relational patterns as they work through the material and the exercises over the course of the sixteen weeks. The authors underscore the attainability of this goal in a chapter that presents empirical support derived from a study of twenty-nine multiply traumatized women who participated in five different groups. Therapists are expected to be active, directive, and goal-oriented. They are encouraged to directly confront group members' traumatic reenactments and offer corrective information that is then tested out with other group members. In this way, participants are assisted in their ability to differentiate past from present and to stop the generalization of schemas about self and others first *in vivo* in the context of the group and then in real-life applications outside of group. The authors appreciate that this therapeutic stance and the direct exposure to traumatic stories and process are anxiety provoking for therapists and they helpfully offer specific information to lessen anxiety and build therapeutic confidence. They have done what they encourage group members to do for one another: use information and the social context to support them. To that end, they devote one chapter to the topic of traumatic reenactments so that therapists are able to anticipate them and see them as opportunities for growth rather than as management problems, and another chapter to therapist competencies and challenges.

This excellent book reflects the authors' dedication and perseverance in helping traumatized women. It is a wealth of carefully honed and clearly presented information designed to both explain the model and sustain the therapists who implement it. *Trauma-Centered Group Psychotherapy* makes an important contribution to the currently evolving treatment models for psychological trauma. I highly recommend it and intend to use it in my practice in the near future.

Christine A. Courtois, PhD
Psychologist, independent practice, Washington, DC;
E-mail: cacourtoisphd@aol.com
Author of Recollections of Sexual Abuse: Treatment Principles and Guidelines *and* Healing the Incest Wound: Adult Survivors in Therapy

Preface

We have designed a model of group therapy for psychological trauma. This model has emerged out of our work with a wide range of traumatized individuals over the past twenty years. Our model is based on a developmental perspective of trauma and its effects. It is designed to be useful for clients who have experienced single traumas in adulthood, as well as for multiply traumatized clients who have also been deeply affected by longstanding abuse and neglect as children. We have found that this model is effective even when group members also suffer from chronic psychiatric illnesses or from different types of traumas. Our model grows out of and also differs from those models already developed (Foy et al., 2002; Herman & Schatzow, 1984; Harris, 1998; Linehan, 1993; Margolin, 1999; Resick & Schnicke, 1993). We have also benefited from the increasing number of empirical studies of group therapy with this population (Alexander et al., 1989; Chard, 2005; Classen, Koopman, Nevill-Manning, & Spiegel, 2001; Cole & Barney, 1987; Goodman & Nowak-Scibelli, 1985; Hazzard, Rogers, & Angert, 1993; Lundqvist & Ojehagen, 2001; Morgan & Cummings, 1999; Najavits, Weiss, Shaw, & Muenz, 1998; Neimeyer, Harter, & Alexander, 1991; Ryan, Nitsun, Gilbert, & Mason, 2005; Saxe & Johnson, 1999; Tourigny, Hebert, Daigneault, & Simoneau, 2005; Wallis, 2002; Zlotnick et al., 1997). The establishment of a diverse range of empirically tested therapeutic models in this field is greatly needed, given the tremendous need for treatment among traumatized women (see Foy et al., 2000 for an excellent overview).

This book describes the application of the Trauma-Centered Group Psychotherapy model in the treatment of multiply traumatized women with heterogeneous traumas (e.g., sexual assault, incest, domestic violence, physical abuse, emotional abuse, physical injury, natural disaster, motor vehicle accidents). Though this model can be applied to other populations, in this book we will present material that is specific to traumatized women. The book begins with a presentation of the theoretical and procedural aspects of the model, then presents in manual form detailed outlines of each therapeutic session. The book concludes by discussing challenging situations. The Appendixes include the client workbook and graduation ceremony. We hope that the material presented here will provide sufficient detail for informed clinicians to apply this model in their clinical setting.

This model has been implemented since 1993 with a variety of populations with PTSD including male veterans, female substance abusers, chronic mentally ill, sexually abused males, and personality disorders. Approximately thirty groups have been conducted over the course of twelve years, with consistently excellent qualitative reports from participants. In addition, a preliminary empirical study of thirty-three women in five groups was conducted, showing significant and enduring reductions in PTSD symptoms and life satisfaction (Lubin, Loris, Burt, & Johnson, 1998). We are hopeful that more research will demonstrate the efficacy of this method.

Acknowledgments

We wish to express our appreciation to our clients, from whom we have learned much. Their courage to confront the terrible events that beset them continues to inspire us and give us hope.

We also wish to thank our many colleagues in the psychological trauma field who have provided encouragement, guidance, helpful criticism, and friendship. Our colleagues at Yale University and the National Center for PTSD, VA Medical Center, offered us the rare opportunity to experiment with a wide range of techniques amidst an exciting and productive academic environment.

Trauma-Centered Group Psychotherapy for Women
© 2008 by The Haworth Press, Taylor & Francis Group. All rights reserved.
doi:10.1300/6097_c

PART I.
THE TRAUMA-CENTERED GROUP PSYCHOTHERAPY MODEL

Chapter 1

Objectives and Rationale

Despite advances in the treatment for posttraumatic stress disorder for women, there remains a significant need to address the interpersonal ramifications of traumatic experience; there is no better place to do so than in group therapy. Trauma is pervasive, intrusive, and lingers near the heart—it takes time for all of its tendrils to wither. After desensitization, education, and medication, comes practice; learning how to apply new means of coping with trauma in a group setting can be a crucial step for women on their journey to recovery. The connection to others that occurs in groups consolidates progress: struggling together with the arising remnants of traumatic schemas, confronting the need to forgive and move on and its counterpart, never forgetting, are the challenges and benefits of group therapy.

Having participated in groups with traumatized women for many years, we know about the triumphs and the failures, and the hard work that goes into both. Acknowledging the profound alterations in perception, personality, and relationships that traumatic experience causes is indeed humbling. The barriers to recovery may seem at times impenetrable, but with time and persistence, we have seen these walls come down. Though this also occurs in individual therapy, engaging the potential power of the group in this task often shows impressive benefits.

The objective of the trauma-centered group psychotherapy (TCGP) model, therefore, is to utilize the power of group dynamics to penetrate the maladaptive patterns of trauma victims. This is accomplished with persistent application of focused techniques, addressing the traumatic events without hesitation, and always showing a deep respect for the strength and tenacity of the distorted traumatic schemas.

Trauma-Centered Group Psychotherapy for Women
© 2008 by The Haworth Press, Taylor & Francis Group. All rights reserved.
doi:10.1300/6097_01

This method has been formerly called "interactive psychoeducational group therapy," but has now been renamed to more accurately portray its methodological principles. The group therapy model is situated within a broader clinical model that we have developed.

TRAUMA-CENTERED PSYCHOTHERAPY

Our general method of trauma treatment is rooted in a developmental theoretical foundation (see Chapter 2) that locates the fundamental injury in an impairment of the capacity for *differentiation,* in sensory, affective, cognitive, and social spheres. Distorted traumatic schemas arise out of this impairment in differentiation. The repair of this injury occurs when distorted schemas are confronted while the client is in a state of imagined exposure to her original traumatic experiences. Due to the continuous and pernicious operation of avoidance, the client's responses to stressors in her current life are shaped by the distorted schemas, leading her into ever-expanding cycles of dysfunctional behavior. The perceived emergencies in her current life are too often fueled by linkages with the pool of fear and anxiety from her original traumatic experiences.

The treatment strategy is based on the assumption that the client, and to some extent the therapist, are continuously using *avoidant* strategies that must be overcome, as well as its corollary that at any given point the client's narrative of her experience is *incomplete.* The therapist is guided by three basic principles: *immediacy, engagement,* and *emotionality.* Immediacy means that the therapist does not wait or hesitate to begin an inquiry about the client's traumatic experiences. Though this inquiry at all times respects the client's perspective, the therapist indicates that accessing the traumatic experience is paramount to successful treatment. Engagement means that the therapist demonstrates to the client an active and engaged interest in her traumatic experiences, and a willingness to be available to the client in her path toward recovery. Emotionality means that treatment is expected to arouse emotion and that the therapist is not fearful of emotional expression. These principles of treatment are applied in individual, family, and group therapies. We now turn to an examination of the unique aspects of group therapy in the amelioration of traumatic stress.

CRITICAL ELEMENTS OF GROUP THERAPY

The group environment is very relevant for traumatized individuals due to their experience of isolation and separation from communal supports that occurs in the midst of trauma (Abbott, 1995). The group serves as a symbolic societal witness to the victim's experience, as it is retold and relived in the group process. Fundamental societal functions, (e.g., securing safety, sharing affective distress, determining basic attributions of responsibility, and welcoming the victim back home) are replayed within the group interaction (Foy et al., 2001; Klein & Schermer, 2000; van der Kolk, 1987). Group therapy provides a corrective emotional experience of the victim's "homecoming," in which inevitable dynamics of self-blaming, loss of credibility, and silencing of the victim are evoked and then worked through (Catherall, 1989; Johnson et al., 1997). The group's intrinsic multiplicity of perspective will highlight differentiated perceptions of each member's traumatic experience, which will allow the individual the important opportunity to integrate her unique history into a revised sense of self without feeling cut off, misunderstood, or rejected by others.

Generally, models of group treatment have varied according to several critical issues: (1) what degree of homogeneity among members is desired, (2) what degree of *exposure* to traumatic memories is demanded, (3) how structured are the treatment sessions, and (4) the *extent of psychopathology* that is tolerated. Let us place the TCGP model within these categories.

Homogeneity

Most clinicians agree that the treatment of posttraumatic stress disorder (PTSD) should begin in a highly homogeneous treatment environment, in which clients experience the safety and security afforded by exposure to others who have had highly similar experiences (Bloom, 1997; Herman, 1992b; Marmar, Foy, Kagan, & Pynoos, 1993; Parson, 1985; Scurfield, 1993). Feelings of isolation, mistrust, and shame among trauma victims may be more readily overcome in the early stages of treatment within homogeneous environments (Parson, 1985). Learning that one is not alone or crazy appears to be of prime importance in the recovery process, and is facilitated by a high degree of similarity among members. Significant differences in experience among members place too great a strain on individual members' capacities for accommodation, and may lead to a high dropout rate (Parson, 1985). Homogeneity helps keep the focus on the trauma, encourages more detailed recall, authorizes the feedback provided by other group members, and minimizes the "we-they" split that often cripples the treatment group (Scurfield, 1993).

Despite the advantage of enhancing group cohesion, highly homogenous groups may also have some negative aspects. Clients may become attached to their identities as victims, delaying their adaptation to the normal world (Brende, 1983; Nicholas & Forrester, 1999; van der Kolk, 1987). Collusive group interactions may occur in order to protect individual members from being singled out, preventing members from taking responsibility or acknowledging certain realities (Parson, 1985). Appreciating member differences and engaging in appropriate interpersonal conflicts are important means toward greater individuation. A group consisting of similarly victimized clients may become too insular, unintentionally increasing the alienation of the clients from their families and society at large (Johnson, Feldman, Southwick, & Charney, 1994; van der Kolk, 1987). Helping victims differentiate their own experiences from others without feeling intense shame or fear may be more likely to occur in heterogeneous groups.

In view of these considerations, a number of authors have proposed treatment models that progress from homogeneous to heterogeneous stages. For example, Herman (1992b) proposes a three-stage model of safety, remembrance/mourning, and reconnection. She recommends individual work in the first stage, homogeneous groups in the second stage, and heterogeneous groups in the third stage. Another model aims to gradually increase members' psychological differentiation and individuation, in which differences among group members are increasingly identified and explored (Parson, 1985). VanDeusen and Carr (2003) have designed a two-stage model that incorporates first supportive and then trauma-focused formats. Johnson et al. (1994) have identified first- and second-generation models for inpatient PTSD treatment, characterized by homogeneity and heterogeneity, respectively. First-generation programs are sanctuarial environments highly responsive to clients' expressed needs (Bloom, 1997), while second-generation programs encourage transactions across various societal and family boundaries, deemphasizing inter-member bonding.

Trauma-centered group psychotherapy utilizes a heterogeneous treatment environment, and thus is aligned with second-generation approaches. The idea behind the formation of a heterogeneous trauma group is to emphasize differences among individuals and to depathologize their experience of the trauma. Traumatized individuals are forced to overaccommodate to the challenges posed during the traumatic moment. Later in their life they tend to continue utilizing overaccommodation as a coping strategy. This behavior is more easily targeted in the context of a diverse group where other group members with different trauma experiences can see the maladaptive aspects of the same coping strategies they are using (Meyer, 2000). The common denominator, hence, is not centered in the type of trauma but rather in the clients' experiences. The more diverse the group the more likely is the possibility to connect to each other based on social principles rather than victim perspectives.

Exposure

Another important consideration in the group work is the timing of the trauma disclosure. It has been a common practice to delay trauma disclosure to a later phase of the treatment after group cohesion and sense of trust have been established. More recently, a number of trauma-focused models have been proposed (Foy, Ruzek, Glynn, Riney, & Gusman, 2002; Spiegel, Classen, Thurston, & Butler, 2004). Empirical research comparing efficacy of trauma-focused versus present-focused models has begun (Classen, Koopman, Nevill-Manning, & Spiegel, 2001; Saxe & Johnson, 1999; Schnurr et al., 2003; Zlotnick et al., 1997).

In the TCGP model, trauma disclosure occurs as early as the first session. An early disclosure prior to the development of group cohesion is possible due to the strong containment experienced in the group through its psychoeducational structure. We believe that the early disclosure not only reduces anticipatory anxiety by overcoming avoidance, but also results in enhancing group cohesion. The experience of safe disclosure so early in the group development sets the norm for trauma-centered work. Because every group member is fully preoccupied with her trauma prior to the commencement of the

group, immediately addressing this preoccupation reduces the anticipatory anxiety associated with such treatment. Our experience over
the past ten years shows a very small dropout and attrition rate, which
we believe is due in part to the use of early disclosure.

Structure of Sessions

Group models vary according to the degree that sessions are structured. Generally, the greater the structure (i.e., attention to time
boundaries, use of lecture, homework, written assignments, organization, and so on), the greater the containment of affect and the
greater control the therapist has over the flow of the group (Fallot &
Harris, 2002; Margolin, 1999). On the other hand, greater structure
requires a task-oriented approach that may interfere with the therapists' ability to listen to the clients, and may suppress important information from them.

The TCGP model falls in the middle on this issue: The beginning
and ending of the session are highly structured and controlled by the
therapist, while the central period is more open for spontaneous interaction and expression of affect. The therapist intentionally titrates the
level of structure during the session to maintain a working level of affect.

Extent of Psychopathology

Many models exclude clients with more severe psychopathology
during the screening process in order to ensure greater stability in the
group (Foy et al., 2000). These kinds of clients typically have dissociative symptoms, severe personality disorders, a history of early
childhood abuse, and usually qualify for the diagnosis of disorders of
extreme stress, not otherwise specified (DESNOS) (Pelcovitz et al.,
1997). Yet these clients are often in the most need of treatment. The
challenge is to be able to provide them with trauma treatment in a
group context in which they will be able to function successfully
(Cloitre & Koenen, 2001).

Our model attempts to provide for (such) clients with multiple
traumas and a broad range of symptoms. Clearly, any client whose
status is actively psychotic, behaviorally violent or out of control, and
who is recently in and out of the hospital, is not a good candidate for
any form of group therapy, including TCGP. However, the more

highly structured group format of TCGP seems to provide sufficient holding capacity to include clients who have chronic and severe symptoms. We have recently successfully extended the use of the TCGP model to clients who have comorbid diagnoses of schizophrenia and bipolar disorder in a community mental health center.

Chapter 2

A Developmental Theoretical Framework

We have found that a developmental perspective is most informative of the alterations in adaptation, personality, and behavior we have observed in our clients with psychological trauma. Although other perspectives (such as biological, learning, and information processing models) provide important insights, the developmental perspective has provided the most flexibility and scope required in our clinical work.

Our developmental model is based on the pioneering work of Bruner (1964), Piaget (1962), Werner (1948), and Werner and Kaplan (1963), and influenced by developmental object relations theorists (Jacobson, 1964; Kohut, 1977; Mahler, Pine, & Bergman, 1975; Winnicott, 1953). Previous references to this developmental perspective are contained in Johnson, Feldman, Southwick, and Charney (1994), Lubin and Johnson (1997), and Johnson and Lubin (2000). We have also been deeply influenced by many of our colleagues in the trauma field who have applied developmental concepts, especially Briere, 1992; Figley, 1985; Green, Wilson, and Lindy, 1985; Herman, 1992b; Horowitz, 1976; Krystal, 1988; Lifton, 1988; McCann and Pearlman, 1990; Roth, Dye, and Lebowitz, 1988; and van der Kolk, 1987.

NORMAL DEVELOPMENT AND THE PROCESSES OF ACCOMMODATION AND ASSIMILATION

We propose that PTSD symptoms and other sequelae of trauma are best viewed as the result of the organism's inability to adapt to the traumatic stressor. An understanding of the nature of the traumatic in-

Trauma-Centered Group Psychotherapy for Women
© 2008 by The Haworth Press, Taylor & Francis Group. All rights reserved.
doi:10.1300/6097_02

jury, therefore, must explain the observed alterations in the person's capacity for adaptation. We will primarily utilize the ideas of Piaget (1962), who analyzes adaptation in terms of two constituent processes: *accommodation,* in which the individual modifies established schemas (motoric, symbolic, and cognitive) in response to environmental stimuli and objects, and *assimilation,* in which the individual incorporates external objects, symbols, or ideas into previously learned schemas. Accommodation leads to learning new schemas, while assimilation leads to new uses of objects. Accommodation represents the primacy of the external world over the internal, and is accomplished largely through imitation. Work is an adult activity that emphasizes accommodation by the person to the demands of the roles and tasks established by the organization. Assimilation, on the other hand, represents the primacy of the internal world over the external, and is accomplished largely through play and fantasy. Imagination and creativity are adult activities that rely on assimilation.

Successful adaptation occurs when these two processes are relatively balanced, providing what Piaget identifies as "the mobility and reversibility of thought" (1962, p. 284). The balanced interaction between self and environment allows for both to be transformed in ways that provide integration of experience, as for example in the development of comprehended language. The elements of language (i.e., letters, words, grammar) are learned through imitation (i.e., accommodation), but are given meaning by linking them to personal associations and images (i.e., assimilation). The result is that one person can communicate inner states of feeling and thought to another. Mobility and reversibility of thought are the basis for concrete operations, by which relations among internal images and external objects can be transformed and manipulated. Through such capacities, the individual develops essential differentiations in perception, being able to perceive different stimuli both as distinct, and as parts of a larger whole. A differentiated perception consists of making *partial* distinctions among feelings, ideas, or events, such that one simultaneously acknowledges both similarities and differences. It is this simultaneity that results in the experience of the *autonomy* of the thought or object. Imbalance between accommodation and assimilation expresses itself in impairment in the individual's capacity for differentiation, resulting in less complex and flexible representations of reality. Inadequate differentiation results in experiencing only the similarities between two entities (leading to a state of overidentification or merging), or only the differences (leading to a state of isolation or dissociation). Piaget's concepts have been extended to an understanding of the regulation of affect (Lane & Schwartz, 1987). The development of flexible and complex cognitive structures allows for processes of symbolization, representation, and mental imagery, all of which are essential to the expression and transformation of states of bodily arousal into experienced emotions. Thus imbalance between accommodation and assimilation also results in a deficit in differentiating affect states, leading to a loss of their regulation.

These developmental concepts have also been applied to the interpersonal dimension by Winnicott (1953), whose concepts of transitional object and transitional space contribute to an understanding of the optimal interpersonal environment for successful adaptation by the child. The transitional space is the intermediary realm between mother and child in which the boundaries between self and other overlap. This "holding environment" provides a relatively safe opportunity for the child to experiment with both accommodating to the external world and assimilating objects into his/her play. If the mother either does not allow the child room to play, or alternatively is too responsive to the child's every need, then the situation becomes imbalanced, and the holding capacity of the transitional space becomes threatened. The development of stable, flexible, and differentiated interpersonal relationships is therefore also dependent upon this critical balancing between accommodation and assimilation.

IMPACT OF TRAUMA
ON DEVELOPMENTAL PROCESSES

The nature of trauma is *forced accommodation,* whether in sudden overwhelming trauma such as rape or severe motor vehicle accident, or in longstanding abusive interactions such as childhood sexual and emotional abuse, in which the perpetrator dominates and controls the response of the victim. In either case, the victim is forced to accommodate to the perpetrator out of fear of harm, abandonment, physical injury, or death. States of intense fear and helplessness shatter the benign environment within which operational thought can exist. Janoff-Bulman's (1992) concept of the *assumptive world* is another name for the benign internal environment/transitional space that is shattered by trauma. A traumatic or abusive experience, we propose, directly interferes with the balancing between assimilation and accommodation. Trauma is overwhelming and incomprehensible exactly because the integration between these two processes is disrupted. Concrete operational thought collapses into its constituent parts. Piaget notes that when the child is "confronted by physical reality extended both in space and time," and cannot achieve comprehension, then "he either assimilates reality to the ego without accommodating to it, or accommodates his activity or his representations without immediately assimilating them" (1962, p. 283). Examples of pure assimilation include dissociation or evocation of previous schemas as a means of resisting the impact of the trauma. Thus, in the midst of the event, people may engage in irrelevant actions such as grooming themselves, singing a childhood song, or calling out for their parents. In contrast, examples of total accommodation in which existing schemas collapse or are altered to match the structure of the event include (1) identification with or attachment to the perpetrator, (2) during combat, giving up notions of oneself as a moral being and becoming a rampaging beast, or (3) after rape, feeling forever soiled. These unassimilated pieces of traumatic experience may then remain beyond words and cognitive representation. They may become split off, and later return as flashbacks and nightmares, or pervade the person's behaviors and self-schemas.

Thus we propose that the etiological root of the psychological injury from trauma is the disruption in accommodation and assimilation. In trauma, the person's capacity to maintain an equilibrium between assimilation and accommodation is destroyed; her body is forced to accommodate to the demands of the perpetrator, natural disaster, or abusive situation, while her mind either succumbs to the new definitions of self and world implicit in the traumatic scenario, or retreats into a pure assimilation of the event via dissociation. It is this profound disruption in equilibrium that causes the core impairment of trauma, namely, lack of differentiation in the resulting traumatic schemas.

Thus we propose that all of the various symptoms, processes, and impairments noted by observers in the trauma field are derivatives of one underlying fundamental impairment in the person's capacity for *differentiation*. Differentiation is disrupted within a limited or more pervasive field of schemas depending upon the state of the person's internal world at the time (vulnerability affected by age, illness, or other stressors), and the degree to which the traumatic situation impacts on diverse areas of meaning and functioning. Over time, however, as the traumatic schemas are applied to new experiences, deficits in differentiation may spread into other areas of a person's functioning, even those not directly associated with the traumatic event.

Our model proposes that the disturbances in differentiation have primary effects, which then over time develop into secondary effects, and finally tertiary effects. Figure 2.1 illustrates this model.

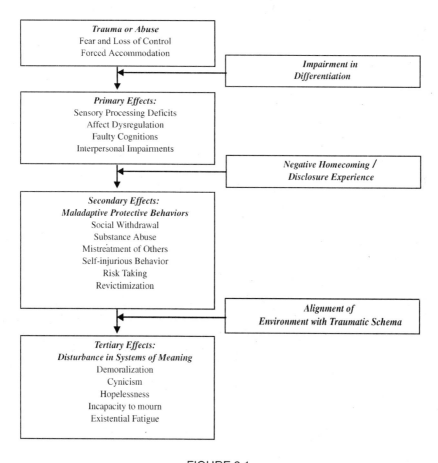

FIGURE 2.1.

Primary Effects of Traumatic Dedifferentiation

Deficits in differentiation affect the person across all dimensions of experience: sensory, affective, cognitive, and interpersonal. Primary symptoms of dysregulation appear in each of these domains in direct relation to the degree of impairment in differentiating capacity. These primary effects include both the essential symptoms of PTSD (reexperiencing, avoidance, and hyperarousal) and some symptoms of DESNOS (affect dysregulation, interpersonal impairments).

Sensory Processing Deficits

The inability to differentiate within the sensorimotor sphere leads to disruptions in perception of internal bodily states (i.e., kinesthetic/proprioceptive sensations) as well as external stimuli (i.e., perceptual sensations). Symptoms include becoming either highly sensitized to internal states of tension, revealed in somatization, conversion symptoms, chronic pain, or highly desensitized, as in derealization, bodily numbing. Dysregulation of perceptual stimuli leads to either reexperiencing symptoms (e.g., flashbacks, intrusive memories), or amnestic and dissociative symptoms.

Affect Dysregulation

Poor differentiation in the domain of affect leads to mood lability because affect states tend to become global, less articulated, and less predictable. Affect may be downregulated, as revealed in emotional numbing, loss of interest, or upregulated, as in hyperarousal symptoms of irritability, startle, insomnia, and hypervigilance (Wolfsdorf & Zlotnick, 2001). The alternation between states of flooding and denial, for example, is another way to describe this process.

Faulty Cognitions

Poorly differentiated cognitions are revealed in many avoidance symptoms, as well as suspiciousness and paranoid thinking. Cognitive-behavioral scholars in particular have identified the importance of faulty cognitions in the avoidant thinking and behaviors of trauma victims (Beck & Emery, 1985; Foa & Kozak, 1986; Resick & Schnicke, 1993). Indeed, many of these faulty thinking patterns (e.g., exaggeration/minimization; disregarding information; oversimplifying; overgeneralizing; mind reading) are clearly examples of impaired differentiation. A differentiated response, such as viewing the rape as only one incident and not one's destiny, demonstrates the capacity for making partial distinctions within a whole, versus global, all-or-none distinctions. Faulty cognitions may also support counter-avoidant ideas, such as those revealed in denial and risk-taking behaviors, in which the victim minimizes the presence of danger (Glodich & Allen, 1998). The term, "either-or thinking," is another description of this process.

Maladaptive Interpersonal Relations

Forced accommodation causes an alteration in the capacity for differentiation in interpersonal relations by linking the original fear response to ambiguities in the boundaries between self and other. Ambiguity in these boundaries evokes the possibility of invasion by the other into the self, and thus must be avoided either through unrealistically impermeable boundary setting (e.g., in detachment, agoraphobia), or through merging with the other (e.g., seen in revictimization, idealization of perpetrator). Thus, in intimate interactions with others, the victim may attempt to protect herself by either being one with others, or being completely separate from others, for then in either case she cannot be singled out. To behave or think independently appears to run a great risk: *to be the only one* who had this particular misfortune. Thus, the dynamics of *pseudocohesion* noted in trauma groups are propelled by fears of differentiation (Parson, 1985; van der Kolk, 1987).

Secondary Effects of Traumatic Dedifferentiation

In response to these primary effects, victims attempt to diminish their symptoms and suffering through *maladaptive protective behaviors*. These secondary adaptations to the trauma may be manifested in various defense mechanisms that serve to dampen, avoid, and contain the disturbing experience, such as projection, reaction formation, and denial, as well as obsessive and avoidant defenses and behaviors. Examples of such behaviors include: social withdrawal, mistreatment of others, revictimization, risk-taking, substance abuse, and self-injurious behavior (Classen, Koopman, Nevill-Manning, & Spiegel, 2001;

Glodich & Allen, 1998; Najavits, Weiss, Shaw, & Muenz, 1998). The degree to which these defensive means are required may be affected by the degree to which the victim experiences a negative (i.e., rejecting, blaming) response from the environment upon disclosure of the traumatic event. Presumably, the inability of the victim to share social defenses against anxiety will lead to greater reliance on personal defenses.

In cases of childhood trauma, these secondary adaptations may affect the interpersonal relationships of the developing child, eventually being incorporated as traits of mistrust, withdrawal, paranoia, self-defeating behavior, or acting out. Employment of these defenses over many years shapes personality development, and may result in permanent alterations in the victim's personality style (Putnam, 1989; Schultz, 1990). In some individuals, these alterations may become autonomous from the original trauma, in the form of a personality disorder, often of the borderline or antisocial type (Lubin, Johnson, & Southwick, 1996).

The application of these protective behaviors usually leads to conflict with the person's environment, assuming that environment is largely more benign and not itself imbued with traumatic schemas. However, in many cases, these maladaptive protective behaviors are not dystonic with those expected by the environment, and alignment develops between the person's traumatic schema and her immediate environment. The greater the alignment, the less discrepant information is presented to the victim, thus supporting the maintenance of the pathological situation. New experiences increasingly are assimilated into the traumatic, suffering picture, resulting in a chronic illness (Bloch, 1987). For example, isolating oneself from others will result in a reduction in the number of friends. Engaging in risk-taking behavior increases the likelihood of being retraumatized. Substance abuse leads to increased inability to regulate affect.

Tertiary Effects of Traumatic Dedifferentiation

The increasing encapsulation of the person within a life structure dominated by and consistent with her traumatic schema inevitably leads to the tertiary effects of disturbances in systems of meaning (e.g., demoralization, cynicism, hopelessness, incapacity to mourn, and existential fatigue). Increased isolation and lack of interaction with her environment, lack of experiences discrepant with her traumatic schemas, and the continued suffering from symptoms and loss of resources, eat away at the victim's remaining efforts to adapt. Unimpeded, the course of illness leads to what has been observed as *posttraumatic decline* (Titchener, 1986), and in the symptoms of DESNOS.

Relationship between Simple and Complex PTSD

The effects listed are nearly identical with those contained within the proposed diagnostic criteria for complex PTSD, also known as DESNOS (Pelcovitz et al., 1997). These criteria were developed phenomenologically based on clinical knowledge of clients with the disorder. The developmental model proposed above predicts these deficits well.

The concept of DESNOS offers a diagnostic formulation beyond simple PTSD that encompasses the complexity of childhood trauma and its long-term sequelae (Herman, 1992a). Depending largely upon the age of onset and duration of the abuse, and subsequent need to utilize adaptational defenses due to an unsupportive interpersonal environment, victims of trauma may experience progressively greater damage to their personality, interpersonal relatedness, and behavior.

In our model, the classic PTSD symptoms of reexperiencing, avoidance, and hyperarousal are among the immediate effects of trauma. The fundamental impairment of differentiation is at first circumscribed around schemas directly linked to the traumatic event. However, as the person applies her traumatic schemas in recursive iterations over time, the impact will be felt in increasingly broader contexts, resulting in the symptom picture of what has been variously termed DESNOS, complex trauma, or more recently developmental trauma disorder (van der Kolk, 2005). Thus it is no surprise that most clients with DESNOS also have PTSD, and this relationship strengthens as time since the traumatic event increases (Roth, Newman, Pelcovitz, van der Kolk, & Mandel, 1997).

The single trauma in adulthood can therefore be seen to be a special case of a larger conceptualization of trauma. In such a case, the discrepancies between pre- and post-trauma schemas may be more defined and less pervasive, and thus easier to address than those that occurred coincident with childhood development. However, DESNOS symptoms are the natural progression of the illness, of which PTSD symptoms are only the first manifestations. The advantages of such a model allow us to conceive of intervention in more than single, adult trauma cases, to include those who have been multiply traumatized, who have developed general psychiatric illnesses, and who have experienced heterogeneous traumas. We turn now to a description of our basic treatment strategy.

TRAUMA-CENTERED GROUP PSYCHOTHERAPY TREATMENT STRATEGY

Aims

Based on the conceptualization, TCGP attempts to intervene at all three levels of impairment. The *primary* effects are treated through interventions that help the client make differentiated responses to challenging situations. This is accomplished within the safety of the therapy setting when traumatic schemas are evoked by distinctions made among members, and then confronted by discrepant information. Group therapy offers many opportunities for work on differentiation due to its inherent multiplicity, no matter how homogeneous the group members appear to be. When differentiation is achieved, members are able to liberate more resources to deal with their symptoms/illness and direct them toward their future life.

In TCGP, the process of differentiating self from the trauma/illness is accomplished in three basic ways. First, the therapists specifically highlight differences among members' experience, trauma histories, or social contexts. The acknowledgement of heterogeneity within the clients' traumatic events replicates the diversity they confront in natural social contexts (e.g., workplace, community, society), providing them with opportunities to practice accommodation to nontrauma schemas. The irrational cognition, "nobody understands me unless they have experienced exactly what I have experienced," is dislodged by the achievement of understanding and support in the midst of a diverse social context.

Second, the therapists actively uncover the unique, human strengths that still lie within the clients and can be revitalized for the pursuit of recovery. Universal human attributes and characteristics such as intellect, resourcefulness, humor, and creativity, although affected by the trauma, are usually preserved. The individual's capacity to be creative, to care for others, and to contribute to society can be rediscovered within the safe interpersonal setting of the group (Bloom, 1997). The result is that unique aspects of their personalities, rather than their traumatic experiences, serve to define them as individuals in the group therapy interaction. It is the conflict between these positive, pretrauma attributes and the trauma schemas that gives rise to symptoms and "stuck points" (Resick & Schnicke, 1993).

Third, and perhaps most importantly, the therapists directly confront the overgeneralized responses of clients during reenactments of traumatic material within the group interaction. Inevitably, during each session one or more members will become sufficiently engaged to reveal their traumatic schemas through interactions with the group and the therapist. The therapist will engage with the client and, through exercises of real-life discovery (e.g., inquiring of all members of the group about their perceptions of the client), confront the client with information incompatible with her traumatic schemas. This process puts pressure on the client to differentiate her response in the moment.

The *secondary* effects are treated through education about the nature of the maladaptive protective behaviors and the need to alter them. Clients are challenged to question whether these protective behaviors are in fact protective, and alternative coping strategies are taught. TCGP utilizes cognitive distancing techniques in an educational format to support members' intellectual understanding of PTSD as an illness process separate from the victim's motivations, personality, or history. Formal instruction about trauma and recovery helps establish a boundary between the illness and the self.

The *tertiary* effects of demoralization and existential fatigue are addressed by attempts to disturb the alignment between social environment and the traumatic schema, to allow newly experienced differentiated responses to establish themselves. This is largely addressed through changes in daily behaviors and in preparation for testimony to friends and family, which occurs during a healing ceremony at the end of the treatment program. For this ceremony, group members actively create a representation of their trauma and present it to an audience of family members and other interested people. The clients' revelation of their traumatic experiences in a public arena serves as a metaphor of mutuality, rather than privacy: the clients no longer hold the trauma alone. Again, self and trauma are differentiated in the service of recovery.

Organization

In the TCGP model, lectures have been organized to address the primary, secondary, and tertiary effects roughly in that order. Thus the lectures in phase one address somatization, affect regulation, faulty cognitions, and maladaptive interpersonal relations, followed in phase two with lectures on maladaptive protective behaviors such as social withdrawal, substance abuse, risk taking, revictimization, and mistreatment of others. Phase three focuses on the tertiary effects of demoralization, hopelessness, and incapacity to mourn. The public ceremony at the end of the program is intended to begin the process of disruption of previously aligned social environments through direct testimony and participation by family and friends.

Education

Providing information about the effects of trauma and its aftermath is an essential aspect of treatment. Placing clients in the role of students concretizes the healing process. Most clients agree that learning is a process of numerous rehearsals and repetitions. Viewing the healing path as an educational process reduces the resistance to learning by trial and error. Using metaphors to illustrate trauma-related material, (e.g., psychological numbing is like scarring of a wound), facilitate the process of learning about the ways that trauma affected them. Posttraumatic responses and symptoms need to be identified and addressed as consequences of the trauma. Often clients view them as part of their personality and style, leading to feelings of shame and inadequacy. When a behavior or personal style is being identified as a symptom or as posttraumatic adaptation, then it becomes impersonal and more available for change. Naming the trauma on a regular basis prevents regression and/or displacement. Keeping the trauma as the center of attention paradoxically decentralizes it, permitting the individual's current life to take center stage.

Experiential Learning

The developmental perspective taken by TCGP lends itself to the valuation of experience-based learning. Other models, such as prolonged exposure, use in vivo or between-session homework to encourage these differentiating encounters (Foa, Rothbaum, Riggs, & Murdock, 1991). The cognitive processing model relies more heavily on in-session homework assignments where faulty cognitions are verbally confronted by the therapist (Resick & Schnicke, 1993).

We have found that among multiply traumatized clients, whose pervasive self-schemas have been dramatically altered over many years, a more interactive, experiential encounter within the group session has been a powerful avenue for encouraging the development of differentiating responses (Yalom, 1976). Educational minilectures evoke the traumatic schema within the group in the here-and-now, allowing the therapist and other group members to teach the client a new response or at least introduce discrepant information to disrupt a traumatic schema. Interpersonal enactments in the group are usually evoked by members' resistance to differentiation, in which they extend their traumatic schemas onto here-and-now interactions with group members or the therapist. Through this projective event, however, the group therapists are given access to the victim's world, which allows them to point out what belongs to the trauma versus what belongs to the client. In so doing, the therapists help the client to reconstruct the disrupted boundary between inner and outer experience. Though this approach introduces a different and perhaps greater demand on the therapist, who must be able to demonstrate the corrective information in here-and-now interpersonal behavior, we believe that the benefits outweigh the challenges.

Chapter 3

Group Therapy Procedures and Rules

CLIENT SCREENING AND ASSESSMENT

The screening process is accomplished through one or two psychiatric interviews between the therapist and each prospective group participant. The therapist must know about the client's trauma and personal history, diagnostic picture, current life situation, readiness for trauma therapy, and understanding of the group therapy process. The screening also provides both the therapist and the client an opportunity to evaluate how they might work together and whether this treatment will be a good match for the client's needs and expectations.

During the screening meeting the therapist reviews the treatment rationale and structure with each prospective group member. The therapist describes the three treatment phases and the graduation ceremony at the end of the program. It is very important to establish the boundaries of the group treatment ahead of time to prevent any resistance that may arise during the group process. Each group member must understand the session structure, the presence of the board, the lectures, booklet assignments, and the ceremony ahead of time.

Group members may have childhood or adult trauma, recent or remote trauma, and isolated or repetitive traumatic experience(s); however, these must be fairly well-defined and articulated. Clients who have only vague feelings that a trauma might have occurred will not benefit from this group experience.

Since the TCGP has a strong learning component it requires that each of the participants is cognitively unimpaired. The screening process excludes clients who are floridly psychotic or who are mentally challenged. Quite often traumatized individuals, primarily with early

Trauma-Centered Group Psychotherapy for Women
© 2008 by The Haworth Press, Taylor & Francis Group. All rights reserved.
doi:10.1300/6097_03

childhood trauma, have a history of thought impairment particularly at times of crisis. Such clients should be distinguished from those with continuous psychotic-level thinking. At all times, the clinician's task is to assess the client's capacity to benefit from this particular group experience.

The screening process excludes any prospective member who is actively or imminently suicidal. A client with chronic suicidal ideation is not excluded. Very often a traumatized individual has chronic suicidal thoughts reflecting existential fatigue. A client with a history of substance abuse is required to demonstrate a sufficient period of sobriety (usually six months) prior to commencing the group treatment. If relapse occurs during the course of the group, then the client's individual therapist is consulted regarding her continued participation.

At the end of the screening process, the therapist will discuss with the client her goals for treatment, and work with her to clearly define specific goals that match the group's aims. In general, a prospective client is encouraged to continue with individual therapy, since we have found that to be supportive of the treatment process. However, a client is not excluded if she is not in individual therapy.

Because TCGP works best when the women have experienced a variety of different types of traumas, the screening process should monitor the overall composition of the group, so as to prevent the predominance of any one type of traumatic experience.

Special Considerations

Clients who dislike group therapy for structural reasons, such as those who find the presence of others to interfere with their time with the therapist, are usually poor candidates. In contrast, clients who are fearful of group therapy because of personal issues of isolation or shame are often excellent candidates.

Clients who have severe narcissistic personality disorder may be challenged in the group setting where the attention is not focused on them. It is helpful to assess this during the screening meeting and to evaluate their capacity to tolerate the group.

Clients with severe dissociative symptoms need to review their experience of dissociating in a group setting. What helps them reestablish connection to the present time? What do they expect of the therapist during such experience? What helped in the past or in their individual treatment? In our experience clients who feel that the therapists are not afraid of dissociation are more likely to have infrequent episodes. Thus the presence of strong dissociative symptoms does not preclude the client from participation in the program.

Another issue to assess during the screening meeting is a problem with authority. The group setting requires the therapist to perform some management functions and, in the educational format especially, to serve as an "expert." Many clients will have issues with the exercise of authority that are directly linked to their traumas, for example, when the perpetrator was in a position of authority. In such cases, authority "problems" will facilitate access to these traumatic scenarios. On the other hand, some clients will be unable to respond within the bounds of the therapists' authority due to personality disorder or social role, as is sometimes the case with clients who are also professionals or therapists themselves. The principle is that if authority issues will be too distracting for the client, group therapy may not be the best treatment option for them.

TREATMENT PHASES

The trauma affects the individual in all domains of her life: her sense of self, interpersonal capacity, and relationship to the world at large. Therefore we believe that trauma treatment needs to target these affected domains. The program is divided into three phases allowing detailed exploration of the effects of trauma in each aspect of the victim's life.

Phase One (Five Weeks)

The task of this phase is to explore the primary effects of the trauma on the individual's kinesthetic, affective, and cognitive domains. This phase begins with each woman reviewing her traumatic events with the group and receiving feedback and support from group members and the therapists. The themes of the educational lectures during this phase are centered on the issues of shame, emptiness, rage, and disturbances in identity. These issues are traced to their origins in the abuse or the traumatic event. The handling of the initial revelations of trauma is a critical point in the life of the group. Case 3.1 is an example of one woman's experience.

Case 3.1: Lisa

Lisa is a forty-eight-year-old married woman with a mixed ethnic background. She was sexually abused by her father throughout her childhood, until she reached puberty. She disclosed the incest to her mother who did not believe her and blamed Lisa for it. Her mother told Lisa repeatedly that she was unlovable and unattractive and for that reason it was unlikely that her father would have wanted to molest her. Lisa believed that her unattractive physical appearance and unappealing personality were justifications for the abuse. She grew up to be an insecure woman who was grateful for any positive exchange she experienced although most of the time she anticipated rejection from the people in her life. Nevertheless, she was able to get married and raise five children. Her parenting skills were good and she was successful in raising well-adjusted and secure children. She had no recollection of her incest and never disclosed any aspect of her childhood to anyone. Recently in the context of work-related stressors she became very depressed and began having nightmares and flashbacks of her abuse. She was horrified and only then disclosed them to her therapist. She noted her withdrawal from her family, particularly from her husband. She was terrified that they might discover her "ugly" history and would reject her the way her family of origin did. The more her fear heightened the more withdrawn and rejecting she became. This behavior caused enormous distress in her family (but primarily to her, as she took pride in being a better mother to her own children). She was referred to the Women's Trauma Program and completed it successfully.

During the first phase of the program she was quiet and very withdrawn. She rarely maintained eye contact with group members or the therapist. After her disclosure of her trauma she received a lot of support from the group who labeled her parents as inadequate. Lisa was surprised to get such a warm response from the group and cast her eyes downward and rocked back and forth in her chair. The therapist asked Lisa if she was expecting the group to respond to her as her mother had—with rejection and humiliation. She nodded in the affirmative but did not raise her eyes. The therapist asked her to ask the group members what they thought of her abuse and how they felt about her. With much effort Lisa was able to ask each group member and to maintain eye contact with each one of them. She received very caring responses and many made a reference to her inner beauty and her capacity to love her children so openly. This experience allowed Lisa for the first time to form a boundary between her traumatic experience and her sense of self. During the next several weeks she became a more animated and spontaneous member of the group. She then disclosed her trauma to her husband who remained very supportive and intimate with her.

Phase Two (Six Weeks)

The task of this phase is to explore the secondary effects of the trauma on the individual's interpersonal relationships and maladaptive protective behaviors. Themes of the lectures include social withdrawal, substance abuse, dumping on others, and risk-taking. Difficulties in relating to others are attributed to the continued application of originally adaptive posttrauma defenses that no longer meet the needs of current relationships. Clients are encouraged to experiment with the freedom inherent in the spontaneous interactions with each other, in contrast to the constraints imposed on them by their rigid traumatic schemas. Phase Two work is illustrated in Case 3.2.

Case 3.2: Susan

Susan's parents separated in her teens. Susan's father, whom she idealized, did not want this separation. Susan was very angry that her mother had entered a new relationship, because she had hoped that her parents would get back together. Shortly after the separation, Susan's father killed the mother's new boyfriend, and then committed suicide. For the past twenty-five years, Susan has barricaded herself in her one-bedroom apartment without any social contact. During phase one, she was quiet but very attentive to the group members. When she reported her trauma to the group, she had reported it without any emotion and as a trivial event. Then during phase two, after the lecture on isolation (session nine), she became activated, asserting that she felt obligated to stay in her "prison," because it was safer that way. When asked how this was connected to her trauma, she unemotionally reiterated the murder-suicide and the pointlessness of marriage. Some group members were curious about her lack of anger. She told the group that she thought her mother was to blame, and wished her father had not died. The therapist asked what she would have preferred to have happened. Susan became tearful, and for the first time expressed her wish that her father would have killed her mother and had been imprisoned for his actions; in this way she would still have him. The therapist asked Susan if her own "imprisonment" was a means to maintain a connection with her father, and with this intervention, identified her accommodation to her traumatic schema. Susan became tearful and then described her trauma in detail. She received substantial support from the group, who advised her "to get out of her jail and begin living." Over the next several weeks, she indeed began to expand her social network, at first with members of the group, and then with some associates at her workplace.

Phase Three (Five Weeks)

The task of this phase is to explore the tertiary effects of trauma, including demoralization, finding meaning in one's life despite the trauma, and the capacity to mourn one's significant losses. Members are encouraged not to avoid acknowledging the damage done, but through mourning and testimony, to find the way toward reparation and renewal in their lives today. In this phase, adaptive coping strategies are explored in sessions, and then practiced outside the group through the use of homework assignments. Methods of empowerment are used to facilitate acceptance and generate meaning. For example, the group is told to design a creative project that reflects their experience in the group. At the end of the sixteen weeks, a special graduation ceremony is held demarcating the completion of the program. Each member of the group is asked to invite people from her support network to serve as witnesses to her graduation. The client's task is to communicate publicly the impact of her traumatic experience on her life and relationships. The degree of disclosure regarding the trauma is determined by the client. The ceremony provides a unique social context where shame and isolation can be symbolically replaced by empowerment and support. Artwork and written material prepared by the graduates are kept in the "Breaking the Silence Book," which is displayed publicly in the group room and is available for future participants. These activities attempt to transform the meaningless and painful events of the trauma into stories and testimonies that can be shared with others rather than carried alone. In so doing, the ceremony breaks the client's private hold on the traumatic event. The creative process serves metaphorically as an act of expelling the trauma from the self-representation.

Case 3.3 is an example of one woman's work through all three phases.

Case 3.3: Ruth

Ruth is now twenty-two years old. At the age of twelve, one year after her parents divorced, she was sexually assaulted by her father during a summer visitation. She felt guilty about the divorce and believed that she deserved the abuse. She committed herself to silence and did not reveal the assault. At eighteen, she presented at a local emergency room with severe PTSD symptoms, but still did not reveal the details of her trauma. She referred herself to the Women's Trauma Program after she saw an ad in the newspaper.

During phase one, Ruth was quiet though attentive to the verbal and non-verbal exchange among group members. As the more verbal members expressed their fear and vulnerability, she acknowledged her difficulties in expressing her feelings and said that she definitely could not share what had happened to her. The group nevertheless encouraged her to begin telling her story. Some group members recalled when they could not speak about their traumas, and yet how relieved they felt by being able to express their pain more openly. Ruth said she felt envious of the courage of those group members who were capable of sharing their traumas. The therapist congratulated her for making her struggle more clear to the group, which would allow the group to help her overcome her fears. She had learned that others felt similar to her even though their traumas were distinctly different. She realized that her silence was one way she had protected her parents from the pain of the divorce. The group pointed out to her that she needed protection from her parents, not the reverse. This insight finally allowed her to tell the group about the sexual abuse during her visitations with her father. She reexperienced intense shame as she spoke about it in the group and it became obvious to everyone that she had blamed herself for the abuse. Over the course of several sessions, she concluded that she could not be responsible for her parents' divorce and, more importantly, that she did not deserve the abuse.

During phase two, Ruth reported that she was able to tell her boyfriend about some aspects of her traumatic experience. She was surprised to find him a sympathetic and supportive listener, and admitted to the group that she had some doubts about the validity of her perception. The therapist asked if she doubted the authenticity of the support of the group. She nodded her head in affirmation. Here her reality testing in the present was impaired by the infiltration of a traumatic schema, namely, that no one would have believed her if she had told them about her father's abuse. The therapist directed her to ask the group in order to verify her suspicion. She asked one member of the group if she really meant what she had said, and received a warm and caring response that countered her suspicion. The therapist asked her if she was willing to question her doubts about people's care for her and accept the support of the group at this moment. She broke into tears and said, "Yes." The group members were excited about her newfound courage and more open approach. She subsequently became an active and supportive group member. She revealed to the group that she had written a play about her ordeal, but until her experience in this group she had been unable to name any of the characters. "Perhaps soon I will be able to give myself a name, too."

During phase three, Ruth became an integrated member of the group process. She appeared brighter and significantly more verbal. She continued to struggle with her tendency to avoid and withdraw, but was increasingly open to feedback from the group, who helped her remain present and connected. At the graduation ceremony, with her mother and boyfriend as witnesses, she revealed her traumatic story publicly through the play she wrote. Each character of her play was read by a different group member, and she functioned as the narrator. Her story was revealed for the first time to her mother, who was filled with tears of pain and pride. In comparison with her initial presentation, Ruth's relationship to her trauma seemed to have changed: she no longer carried the burden alone.

GROUP PROCEDURES

Overview

A strength of the TCGP model is its ability to provide a safe, containing environment for the highly emotional and arousing recollections that arise. This is accomplished by its highly structured format and the consistency with which the clinician follows it each week. In this way, clients learn to expect it and rely on it for comfort. Each group always starts with a minilecture lasting ten minutes, followed by a process discussion, approximately seventy-five minutes, and ending with a wrap-up during the last five minutes of the session. The beginning and ending of the group are somewhat formalized, to highlight the containing function of the treatment. Thus no informal checking-in or discussion with the clinician ensues prior to the minilecture, and similarly, the clinician exits immediately after the wrap-up lecture. The minilecture and wrap-up lecture provide important cognitive distancing for group members that aids in containing their emotional arousal and heightened vulnerability. These defenses help to prevent the regression that is often seen at the boundaries of the group sessions as members anticipate either the arrival or departure of the therapist. Following these guidelines will contribute greatly to a successful group experience.

The group meets weekly for ninety-minute sessions over a sixteen-week period. Each session begins with a brief minilecture (about ten minutes) followed by an interactive discussion, and then ending with a brief, cognitively oriented wrap-up. Booklets containing the series of lectures are given out at each phase, and homework for each session is assigned. (This booklet is included in Appendix B.) The role of homework is to keep members thinking about the group material between sessions. The homework assignments are optional and are not reviewed during the group meetings. Clients may or may not bring in the homework material to the next session during the process discussion. The therapist uses a board to highlight essential points in the lecture. This educational format initially creates emotional distance. The board and its contents function as an externalizing defense for group members to more safely explore the traumatic material. Soon, however, the open discussion challenges particular members of the group, based on their particular traumas or defenses. Other group members who feel empowered by their newly acquired knowledge may confront these clients' responses in a supportive way. These enactments are usually experienced as beneficial to both parties: some feel effective by providing encouragement and guidance, while others experience the group's efforts at support.

Frequently, the therapist's direct interaction with the clients during the discussion symbolically parallels a traumatic theme. The therapist functions as a witness to the traumatic material, and may be experienced both as the accepting caregiver, as well as the unhelpful bystander who looks on while the victim is being harmed. In either case, the victim's traumatic schema is extended out to include the therapist or group members, usually in an attempt to ward off recognition of the trauma as a past event. Paradoxically, in this moment the victim allows the group into her privately held world. During the enactment, the therapist can alter these schemas by making clear distinctions between the person and the trauma, and between the present and the past. The therapist uses such an enactment to help the clients transform their own isolation into a capacity for bonding. Both the group members and the therapists are available as witnesses to share the burden of the trauma with the individual client. During these moments of enhanced emotional arousal and vulnerability, previously protected emotions are often expressed. Chapter 4 will discuss the management of these moments in more detail.

Toward the end of the session, the therapist returns to the board and gives a brief wrap-up that again provides emotional distancing, and permits closure without an abrupt termination of the discussion. Often group members will remain in the room after the therapist departs, and continue to talk with one another.

Minilecture

The function of the minilecture is to introduce trauma-related topics within the context of the cognitive distancing provided by the educational format. The purpose is to evoke trauma schemas that may interfere with adaptive coping and functioning. The role of the minilecture is twofold. One is to provide a cognitive frame where traumatic themes can be explored. Stimulating members' intellects helps them utilize human resources that are not affected by the trauma. Having an understanding of symptoms or common responses to trauma is reassuring to many clients. By acquiring new information about their condition, women feel more empowered to handle the challenges associated with the recovery process. It is not unusual for group members to learn to name and describe emotions that previously were only experienced somatically. Using an intellectual construct helps the client to contain the feelings that are associated with the trauma. The members who experience this kind of intellectual empowerment usually feel excited about the process and are more hopeful that it will help them to heal. The second role of the minilecture is to evoke traumatic schemas within the members. This nearly always occurs as the members begin to discuss the lecture and voice different or conflicting ideas. The subsequent demand for differentiation will be the mechanism that brings forth various traumatic schemas in certain group members. This allows the group to quickly engage in trauma-centered work during the process discussion that follows. What is important for the therapist to remember is that the presentation of material in the minilecture has a dual purpose: simultaneously imparting information and evoking conflict. The therapist does not try to argue or convince members of the points made in the lecture, but rather waits for the expression of distress that inevitably arises, in order to begin the trauma-based exploration. As the therapist discusses the issue, aspects that conflict with the trauma- (or perpetrator-) based thinking within a client will become evident in the physical or verbal responses of the clients. Therefore, the therapist maintains eye contact with all group members to identify subtle reactions that signal the evocation of a traumatic scenario.

Process Discussion

The minilecture sets the groundwork for the process discussion, which makes up much of the group time, and where much of the therapeutic intervention occurs. The minilecture's goal is to evoke traumatic schemas that tend to interfere with current life interactions and performances. Such interferences that soon arise become the focus of the therapeutic work. The therapists allow a short pause after the lecture for spontaneous expression by group members in response to the topic. Sometimes the group will be silent and the cotherapist or the therapist will need to call on a group member who appears to be affected by the lecture. Signs that indicate the emergence of a traumatic schema include change of facial expression or body posture, downcast eyes, rocking, staring, dissociating, tearing, showing fear or anxiety, or rigid interaction between a group member and the therapist or between two members. The process begins when the therapist acknowledges what she observed, as in Case 3.4 from session eight: Your Body is not Your Enemy.

Case 3.4: Rachel

THERAPIST: Rachel, I noticed that your body tensed up during the lecture.

RACHEL: I feel very anxious.

THERAPIST: Where do you feel the tension in your body?

RACHEL: In my chest and in my neck.

THERAPIST : I wonder if talking about the body as an enemy reminds you of your abuse?

RACHEL: (downcast eyes and tearing) Yes.

THERAPIST: When you were a child and your grandfather took you to the basement, during the abuse, where did you feel the tension in your body?

RACHEL: I remember his weight on my chest and feeling suffocated.

THERAPIST: So who was the enemy?

RACHEL: My body betrayed me. I could not move, my chest was so heavy.

THERAPIST: Rachel, your body responded to the abuse. It is your grandfather who betrayed you. He was not supposed to hurt you.

RACHEL: (crying openly) I don't know.

THERAPIST: Rachel I want you to look up and ask each group member what she thinks about your belief that your body betrayed you.

Rachel proceeded with visible effort to ask each one that question. She received very warm and supportive responses from each of them. Other group members were able to emphatically stress Rachel's innocence and her grandfather's accountability.

THERAPIST: Rachel, do you believe what the group members told you?

RACHEL: Yes.

THERAPIST: Can you repeat that statement yourself?

RACHEL: (shaky voice) It was not my fault.

In this example the therapist detected the body tension that signified the emergence of the traumatic experience, that is, the incest by the grandfather. The therapist assisted Rachel to form the connection between the current symptom/physical reaction and the past abuse. Rachel was not able yet to differentiate the past traumatic experience from her current appraisal of her body, viewing it as her enemy. By asking Rachel to confront her traumatic schema by listening to others' perceptions, she was able to begin to receive support and change a faulty cognition. This exchange allowed Rachel to differentiate between the present and the past and between the self and the trauma.

The therapist's goal is to uncover the underlying traumatic experience that infiltrates the current exchange. The therapist then highlights the difference between the circumstances of the past trauma and the moment. The way in which the therapist accomplishes this task is by asking the woman to challenge her own fear-schemas. If, for example, her fear is that she will be humiliated the same way she was during the abuse then the therapist asks her to ask the group members how they feel about her, or their response to her trauma. Inevitably, the woman receives supportive and caring responses that confront her original rigid idea that she will be humiliated.

The process of tracking a trauma reenactment to its origin accomplishes two goals. One is to gain entry to the inner experience of the traumatized individual and to subsequently alter her traumatic schema. By confronting the rigid traumatic schema while the person's level of arousal is heightened makes the intervention more powerful and effective. The second goal is to demonstrate to the other group members how traumatic schemas distort their perceptions of the world, and that they can be changed. Witnessing this process is very powerful for the entire group because they see the victim actually confront the trauma/perpetrator directly without coming undone or being annihilated. Other members can witness the competence of the therapist in guiding one member through the terror of recollection. Performing this task competently enhances the group's trust in the therapist and in the therapeutic process. The therapist's capacity to tolerate the fear and anxiety that arises helps the group members identify skills they need. It also assures members that dealing directly with their trauma can lead to positive outcomes and therefore they are less likely to avoid the task. The emergence of a traumatic schema can occur immediately after the minilecture as a result of the theme of the lecture or it can occur any time during the discussion process as a result of the discussion itself evoking an aspect of the trauma by the therapist or other group members. Regardless of the timing the therapist needs to acknowledge the reenactment. Failure to do so communicates support for avoidance and silencing.

It is important to recognize traumatic replay that presents in covert ways. A client may express positive sentiments and enthusiastically support the group's rules and norms, eliciting a positive response from both therapist and group members. It is particularly tempting for the therapist not to challenge this behavior, since it is a nice break from the more confrontational interactions with other group members. Yet often these positive behaviors are linked to that person's traumatic experience, for example, in acting in compliance with the perpetrator, and therefore should not be overlooked. Case 3.5 illustrates this point.

Case 3.5: Lynn

LYNN: I always feel anxious at work even though I am a very good worker.

THERAPIST: What makes you so anxious?

LYNN: I am constantly worried that I will make a mistake and my boss will be disappointed in me.

THERAPIST: And what will happen if your boss will be disappointed?

LYNN: (tearing) I don't know. I never get to this point.

THERAPIST: I wonder if you are crying now because you could not answer my question?

LYNN: I try hard to do well.

THERAPIST: What happened when you felt you disappointed in your father?

LYNN: If I was not good all the time he became more denigrating to me in addition to the abuse (molestation).

THERAPIST: What did he say or do?

LYNN: (crying) He called me names, told me I was good for nothing and that I'll never amount to anything.

THERAPIST: I am not your father, Lynn, and I will never put you down or humiliate you. You don't need to try so hard to please me. I am already happy with you as you are.

LYNN: I am so worried all the time that you will be angry at me if I will not be positive.

THERAPIST: I am happy that you shared this issue with us. It must be hard work.

LYNN: I feel exhausted all the time.

THERAPIST: It is time to take care of Lynn.

Lynn appeared significantly less anxious. She received positive feedback from the group members who congratulated her for her courage in sharing her struggle with them.

Here the therapist helped Lynn differentiate between her past attempt to protect herself from her father (the perpetrator) and her relationship with a perceived authority figure (the therapist).

Wrap-Up Lecture

The function of the wrap-up lecture is to summarize the main learning points of the process discussion and to provide cognitive distancing to contain the emotional arousal, in the service of bringing closure to the group. Since the wrap-up is an expected, almost ritualized, structure, group members begin to rely on its use of intellectualization to gain distance from their feelings in preparation for leaving the group space. The use of the impartial board contributes to the reduction of emphasis on interpersonal interaction. The therapist, meanwhile, retreats from being the projected subject (e.g., the perpetrator, the victim, or the bystander), becoming again the educator. In this role the therapist can more easily exit the room, leaving the members with each other and the board. Transitioning the group space into a classroom atmosphere and the rapid departure of the therapist prevent regression. Occasionally a group member must be assessed. In that case the therapist may come back to the group room shortly after departing and call for this member to be evaluated in a different space. It is important to communicate to the group that the therapist is concerned about a distressed member, but without doing so in front of the group at the end of the session.

GROUP RULES

The group rules in TCGP are similar to most group principles that govern such work. These include maintaining respectful behavior, committing to regular attendance, abstaining from alcohol or drug use, and signing a treatment contract (see Appendix C). The rule that deserves special attention relates to social contact outside of group meetings. The TCGP model allows such contact to take place under the agreement that discussion about other group members' issues is prohibited. A direct discussion about their lives and treatment among the individuals who are in contact is encouraged. The rationale for this rule is that profound isolation and withdrawal characterizes the social repertoire of this client population. Some never developed appropriate social skills and others refrain from using them as a result of their fear. We believe that any opportunity to challenge these maladaptive coping skills and any attempt to reconnect socially with another person should be supported and encouraged. Prior to the beginning of the group the therapist clearly reviews the importance of widening their support network and the rationale for allowing social contact outside of sessions, if they choose it. Group members are expected to notify the therapist if the safety of another group member is involved, such as suicidality or self-harming behavior. It is made clear that these communications to the therapist are not acts of betrayal by a member. Our experience has demonstrated that allowing such social contact has not distracted members from the therapeutic work, and in some cases has led to the formation of long-lasting relationships.

The other concept that deserves clarification is the notion of confidentiality. We do commit to confidentiality, however, we stress to the group members that keeping their trauma confidential protects the perpetrator and therefore they should share it with others. They are provided with the opportunity to share their testimonies publicly at the end of the program during the graduation ceremony. This practice of disclosure and sharing of the burden is practiced throughout the treatment.

Chapter 4

Managing Traumatic Reenactments

This chapter will focus in more detail on the handling of traumatic re-enactments during the process discussion. These moments are certainly the most important and most challenging for the therapist, requiring some practice and skill (Hegeman & Wohl, 2000). Generally, experience in working individually with trauma clients will provide the clinician with sufficient background to successfully manage these moments.

Trauma reenactments are corrective experiences only if the therapist engages with the traumatic schema of the client. First the therapist must detect the emergence of a traumatic reenactment. Then the therapist has to communicate to the group member that indeed she is dealing with a trauma reenactment. Calling it a trauma replay establishes a boundary between the past and the present and between real and reexperienced. The therapist must actively reassure her that she is not going to be harmed again and that those feelings and thoughts are coming from the past. Other group members often participate in the process of differentiating the past from the present. The experience of such powerful distortion of the moment within a traumatic reenactment provides the other group members an opportunity to understand the thrust of the healing process.

PREPARATION

It is important that the therapist prepare for these reenactments, for they are an unavoidable and essential part of the therapeutic process. Too often the clinician views them as "failures of containment," a sign of bad technique, or "derailing," requiring bringing the client

Trauma-Centered Group Psychotherapy for Women
© 2008 by The Haworth Press, Taylor & Francis Group. All rights reserved.
doi:10.1300/6097_04

back to reality so that the therapy can continue. In contrast, we view these moments as the best time to act, as windows into the traumatic schema of the client, where change can be most efficiently accomplished.

It is also essential to prepare the group members for these reenactments, to predict their occurrence, and to inform members that these will be important opportunities for healing and not to be afraid of them. By preparing group members ahead of time, the therapist will have less anxiety and confusion to handle when the reenactments occur, when there is much to do.

SPECIFIC STEPS

Once a traumatic reenactment has begun and is identified by the therapist, the first step is to *engage with the client*. This usually means speaking to her, orienting your body toward her, and inquiring about what she is experiencing in the moment. The second step is to *label her experience* as reliving her trauma, as coming from the past, as viewing the present in terms of the trauma. Sometimes it is necessary to mention the relevant aspect of the past trauma that parallels her current perception. The purpose is to directly introduce the differentiation between past and present. The client will almost always express disagreement or puzzlement over the therapist's statement, a stance that should be expected. The next step is to *state that her perception is incorrect,* which directly confronts her with a discrepancy. Expect an increase in tension at this point, since a client will not easily abandon her view. Your aim is not to have her agree with you, but to introduce into her thinking alternate and discrepant points of view that, over time, she can utilize to contain or diminish the impact of her traumatic schema. It is essential that the therapist, in this moment of disagreement, be relaxed, caring, friendly, and intimate. The therapist demonstrates that he or she is not particularly threatened by conflict, that the feedback is a gift, and that the disagreement is an outstretched hand.

Nevertheless, the client will inevitably not agree, so the fourth step is to have her *test it out with the group members*. The therapist asks the client if she would be able to ask all group members to tell her their perception of her behavior or of the issue involved. The therapist then coaches the client to ask each member in turn, and if necessary, prevents the client from interrupting or diverting this feedback. The therapist may ask, "Did you hear what Sheila just said to you?" At the end of this go-around, the therapist may sum up the feedback, again labeling the client's experience as having been affected by her trauma, and therefore as being incorrect in terms of the present. The client may appear influenced by these remarks, or may not. The therapist should reiterate the discrepancy between perceptions without necessarily working to get acquiescence from the client.

The fifth step is for the therapist to *refer to the minilecture and the board* in order to contain affect and to reduce the interpersonal demand of the discussion. This may then lead back into the general discussion, or to another client who has made an important comment that can be explored. Cases 4.1 and 4.2 are two examples that illustrate these steps.

Case 4.1: Jean

Jean was sexually abused by her grandfather for many years during her childhood. The sexual abuse was violent and accompanied by denigrating and humiliating remarks. Jean stared at the ceiling while the abuse took place, which helped her reduce the overwhelming feelings of emotional and physical pain. In the group, as another member was revealing a particularly upsetting memory, Jean began to stare at the ceiling. The therapist remarked that Jean was staring and asked her to describe how she was feeling (*step one: engage with the client*). Jean replied, "I just feel pain." The therapist then pointed out to Jean that she had stared at the ceiling when she was abused as a child, and asked her if the shame she had felt then was linked with vulnerable feelings she was experiencing now (*step two: label her experience*). Jean continued to stare and became tearful. The therapist pointed out to Jean that, unlike before, she was safe now and that her pain was coming from the past (*step three: state that her perception is incorrect*). Jean shifted her eyes downward. The therapist then encouraged her to make eye contact with each member of the group (*step four: test it out with group members*). With great difficulty, she established eye contact with each group member, all of whom made supportive and caring remarks to her. The therapist then reiterated to Jean what had happened, and then referred to the board to underscore the importance of making a differentiation between the time of the abuse and the present—a time when it was now safe to look at others (*step five: refer to the board*).

Case 4.2: Jane and Mary

This example illustrates how to handle a situation in which two women simultaneously have a traumatic reenactment. Jane grew up in a chaotic household. Her parents were immigrants who refused to learn English or to assimilate into the American culture. The family was isolated without any contact with the immediate community where they lived. The mother told the children never to let anyone know about their family problems and that they should keep "the dirty laundry" at home. Jane was significantly younger than her only sister. She looked up to her sister and admired her. Her sister was burdened by the numerous chores she had, including watching Jane. Jane's father was an alcoholic who was violent and belligerent. Her mother was unavailable and withdrew from her children. She told Jane that she had been a mistake and that she was tired of raising children. Jane turned to her sister for support and guidance. Jane admitted to the group that she loved her father and although when he was drunk he was violent, he was the only one who paid any attention to her. She also recalled that when he was sober he spent time with her and she felt loved. Her older sister began drinking heavily during her early teens. At that point she became violent and abusive to Jane. Jane reported to the group that her sister started sexually abusing her at that time. She hated her sister and felt completely betrayed by her. During the third phase of the program Jane decided to disclose to the group the sexual abuse by her sister. This was the first time in her life that she disclosed it, especially to a group of women. When she disclosed it she received warm support from group members. Jane told the group that she forgave her father but she could never forgive her sister. She also admitted to the group that her father was sexually inappropriate with her sister but she was not sure of the extent of the sexual abuse. Jane criticized her sister's alcoholism and held her responsible for her actions toward her.

At that point, unexpectedly, Mary angrily attacked Jane about her lack of sympathy with her sister's pain and ordeal. Mary grew up in an alcoholic household. Her mother drank heavily in her room while the father sexually abused Mary starting when she was six years old. When Mary became an adolescent she started drinking heavily as a way of coping with her pain and the ongoing abuse. The more she drank the more she was able to silence the pain but in addition the more she felt guilty for her failing performance at school. She was blamed for her irresponsible behavior and was reprimanded by both the school authority and her parents. When Mary detected the blaming by Jane of her sister she was no longer able to support Jane in her attempt to repair her wounded relationships with women. The anxiety level in the group was very high. The therapist first asked Jane about her perceptions, and Jane said she experienced Mary as unsupportive and concluded that indeed women could not be her friends. The therapist then asked Mary, who said she experienced Jane as the collaborator in her abuse scenario (*step one: engage the clients*). The therapist then stated that the interaction between Jane and Mary had triggered a reenactment of their respective traumatic events (*step two: label their experience*). Due to the high anxiety in the room, the therapist used the board to demonstrate the reenactment and announce that as a result the "perpetrator" had been evoked in the group. The therapist told Jane that she experiences Mary as her sister, the perpetrator, who in reality is another victim of abuse (*step three: state that the perception is incorrect*). Jane was able to consider it. The therapist asked her if she could listen to Mary some more (*step four: test it out with group members*). Mary said to Jane "maybe if you can understand my pain and that I was not responsible for it you can forgive me and find forgiveness in your heart for your sister's shortcomings. You did not deserve that treatment from her but neither did she from your father." Jane became tearful and said she could understand Mary, but that it was very hard to forgive her sister. The therapist then turned to Mary and said that she had incorrectly experienced Jane's comments as blaming her. "You were the one blamed, though you were the victim" (*step three: state that the perception is incorrect*). Mary argued with the therapist that she thought she was just trying to give Jane some feedback about her lack of forgiveness. The therapist countered by challenging her to find out from Jane and the other group members if they thought Jane would blame her for her past behavior (*step four: test it out with other group members*). Mary became flushed, but nodded. Jane and other group members spoke with great warmth to her about how horrible her situation had been, and that she had been put in an untenable position. Mary burst into tears, revealing her deep need to be forgiven, and her acceptance of the feedback. Jane then again welled up with tears and said how much she had been impressed with Mary's strength and intelligence, and that she had previously hoped that they might become friends. The therapist then again summed up this complex but healing interaction, referred to the board, and made comments about the courage it takes to open oneself to intimate relationships with others (*step 5: refer to board*).

SUMMARY

Once the therapist fully understands the importance of these traumatic reenactments, and accepts their occurrence as opportunities for growth rather than indications of technical failure, they can be effectively managed by following the five steps described above. It is in these crucial, spontaneous, intimate moments that the therapist, representing the present, faces down the trauma and attempts to loosen its hold on the client. The use of feedback from group members in addition to the authority of the therapist serves to introduce a questioning attitude within the client regarding her traumatic schema. We have found that the mere insertion of this discrepancy into her thinking can, over time, begin the unraveling process that ultimately aids in recovery. It is through the intensity and immediacy of these reenactments that the concepts presented in cognitive form come alive and are taken in by our suffering clients.

PART II.
SESSION-BY-SESSION LECTURE SERIES

Chapter 5

Phase I Sessions

Each group session will be described according to the TCGP format: (1) main points: (2) minilecture; (3) process discussion; (4) wrap-up lecture, and (5) potential challenges. Each lecture contains a summary of the main points of the lecture. Feel free to adapt this material to your specific group, setting, and personal style.

The first lecture of each phase sets the thematic tone for each phase. Due to the heterogeneous nature of the group's composition, (e.g., childhood versus adulthood trauma, interpersonal versus impersonal trauma, familial versus nonfamilial), various aspects of each lecture may relate more directly to one or the other aspect. Be sure to make an effort to include all participants by asking them to relate to the lecture material. We have found that sometimes the most productive work arises when the lecture material does not directly coincide with participants' experience, being itself a source of difference. Nevertheless, many of the core experiences of being traumatized are universal and it is rare that a lecture is irrelevant to someone in the group.

SESSION 1: DISCLOSING THE TRAUMA

1. Main Points
   a. Review group rules.
   b. Review treatment phases.
   c. Group members reveal their traumatic experiences.
2. Minilecture
   Hand out and review group rules.
   Hand out Phase I booklets.

Trauma-Centered Group Psychotherapy for Women
© 2008 by The Haworth Press, Taylor & Francis Group. All rights reserved.
doi:10.1300/6097_05

Review program structure on the board and briefly describe the content of each phase of the program:

Phase I—primary effects of trauma on the self   5 weeks
Phase II—maladaptive protective behaviors   6 weeks
Phase III—effects on meaning and mourning   5 weeks
Graduation Ceremony

Refer to Figure 5.1 to explain the three main topics of the program.
3. Trauma Disclosure

Introduce each group member. Ask each one to tell the group about her current life situation (who she lives with, work, relationship, children, therapy) and why she is here. Then each group member is asked to describe the traumatic event (level of disclosure will vary among group members; make sure each one of them at least names her trauma and the main participants).Introduce yourself; describe your background in working with traumatized individuals, training, and other experiences. No personal disclosure is expected. Your introduction should come last to prevent modeling of limited personal introduction. You should introduce yourself by name at the very beginning.
4. Wrap-Up

Acknowledge the level of anxiety that people must have experienced. Reiterate the importance of dealing with all aspects

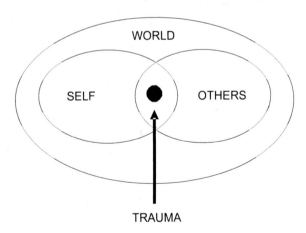

FIGURE 5.1.

of their life, as the trauma has affected them in all domains of life. Make reference to the illustration on the board and emphasize that you will be working with them on these issues over the next sixteen weeks.

SESSION 2: SHAME AND IDENTITY

1. Main Points
   a. Trauma causes a sense of helplessness and powerlessness.
   b. These states lead to shame.
   c. Victims attribute the experience of the trauma to themselves.
   d. Traumatic experiences cause emotional scarring which reduces the person's inner resources.
2. Minilecture

The overwhelming state of helplessness and powerlessness that characterizes the traumatic moment, particularly if the trauma occurs early on in life, leaves the victim with an enormous sense of inadequacy and self-blame. The cognition of "I must be a bad person if my parent is treating me this way" is a distortion of the recognition that the parent is doing something bad to you. When the traumatic experiences are repetitive and ongoing, such as childhood abuse, there are multiple moments of shame and self-blame. Over the years, multiple emotional scars are formed that deplete the individual's resources and capacities for self-care. Even when the trauma occurs later on in life, the profound experience of losing one's capacity to protect oneself and not having control of oneself leads to erosion in the sense of self-efficacy or self-reliance. This erosion also creates scars that deplete the resources that she may have already had.

(Use the analogy of Swiss cheese. Ask them what they notice when they look at Swiss cheese? Redraw Figure 5.2 to illustrate your reasoning.) Right. There are many holes and there is less cheese. If we use this analogy to demonstrate these scars, then the cheese represents the person's internal resources while the holes represent the scars resulting from the trauma. The dark spots are the injury of each trauma; around each the person builds a wall of defense in order to protect herself from the anxiety caused by the trauma. Unfortunately, this requires resources that should be used for other purposes; thus, the trauma indi-

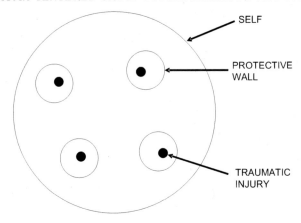

FIGURE 5.2.

rectly eats away at the self. This feeling of "being less than I was" is just another way of describing *shame*.

These multiple scars affect the person's emotional experience, thoughts, interpersonal style, and behavior. Therefore they affect the person's identity or personality. It is not surprising to hear a traumatized individual say "since the trauma I am a different person." Her inner experience becomes shaped by the trauma; in some ways she becomes "It": shameful, bad, disgusting, inadequate, and good for nothing.

3. Process Discussion

(Sit down and allow members to react.)

4. Wrap-Up

Since we cannot change history or take the trauma away, what can we do now to liberate more resources from the hold of the trauma? How can you make more room for *you*? What can be changed in this picture? Exactly. If you remove the walls or the defenses you put up as a result of the trauma, you can make more room inside you, and therefore make yourself more available for positive experiences. These walls served you well for a long time; they protected you when danger was there, namely during and immediately after the traumatic moment. However now they wall you in and burden your every step. You have become a prisoner of your own traumatic past.

(Erase the inner circles to illustrate your point.) Now you have more substance than holes (a reference to the Swiss cheese analogy). You also have more resources to deal with life's challenges and blessings.
5. Potential Challenges

"I'm afraid to let down these walls."

Response: Restate that these walls were needed when danger was present. Now these walls interfere with your life and stand in the way of your future.

"I'm too afraid to change now."

Response: Change is scary. If you were not ready for change, you would not be here in this group. In any case, these changes could not be as difficult as having lived through the trauma!

SESSION 3: THE VOID AND EMPTINESS

1. Main Points
   a. Trauma creates a sense of hollowness or a void.
   b. Trauma overwhelms the victim's coping skills.
   c. Maladaptive coping skills lead to a larger void.
2. Minilecture
   Trauma is a black hole or a sinkhole that takes things away, depletes the person's resources, and creates a sense of hollowness. The darkness of the trauma keeps the person frightened. Often a traumatized individual feels as if she is the walking dead, a zombie. This feeling of deadness marginalizes and alienates her from her family and the community. Think of a person as a container from which a person derives resources, energy, and the essence of life. If the trauma creates a hole in this container, then a void forms, and eventually the person feels empty. What an overwhelming feeling—"just empty"—frightening! The experience of emptiness is intolerable, so often a traumatized individual will naturally attempt to fill the void so she will not feel the emptiness. What are some things you have

filled the void with? (List answers on the board: alcohol, drugs, food, sex, etc. Then draw Figure 5.3 to illustrate your point.)

Yes, in the beginning filling the void with food or alcohol may distract you from the feeling of emptiness. The problem is that its effects are brief. Over the years more is needed in order to fill this void. The void gets bigger, which causes more pain. The more pain you experience the more pressure you feel to fill the void. More booze, more food, more sex! A vicious cycle is created that fuels itself. The trauma is no longer needed to activate it! After all, the danger is over. Now it is your fear of the void that activates this behavior, interferes with your life, and maintains the pain. (Draw Figure 5.4 and demonstrate this vicious cycle.)

3. Process Discussion
4. Wrap-Up

In order to break the vicious cycle you need to remember that the void was created by the trauma. The void is not who you are; it is how the trauma affected you. However, you can affect it. The way to fill a hole is to replace what was lost; that is what we mean by repair. Alcohol and food do not replace lost love or caring relationships; new caring relationships do. Sex does not re-

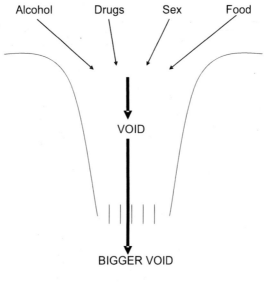

FIGURE 5.3.

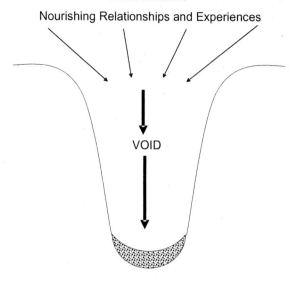

Nourishing Relationships and Experiences

VOID

FIGURE 5.4.

place the peace lost by violence; peaceful experience does. Only by knowing what was lost—through remembering and knowledge can one find the right things to fill the void. If you are hungry, eat; if you were poorly cared for, find someone to care for you. You can do it.

5. Potential Challenges

"Feeling empty is intolerable, even for a moment."

Response: This feeling is a normal human response to the hollowness that the trauma created. Feeling this way makes you human, but it stands in the way of moving on. You had to tolerate a lot during the abuse so it is understandable why you do not wish to tolerate anything that relates to the trauma. But that is why you must find good experiences to help you tolerate it.

"Alcohol and food do take away this feeling."

Response: Of course they help. If they didn't, you wouldn't use them. But for how long? Not long, so you have to keep using them. But why do you want to stop them? Exactly! They are making things worse. In the beginning perhaps they did work well, but now the price is larger than the benefit. What price are you paying? (For example, addiction, job loss, relationship loss, health problems, overweight, worsening of symptoms.)

SESSION 4: MOVING FROM RAGE TO FORGIVENESS

1. Main Points
   a. An unwritten contract of safety exists in any human relationship.
   b. When this contract is broken, one feels mistrust, suspicion, and anger.
   c. These feelings lead to withdrawal from current relationships.
   d. Applying forgiveness to current relationships is essential to healing.
2. Minilecture

   Every person makes the assumption that she will be treated well by others. In order to make connections with others, you must assume that it is safe to do so. This unwritten contract among people needs to be respected by all. If you did not make this assumption, most of us would stay home and avoid all relationships. We must assume it is safe to be vulnerable within a relationship with others. Most of the time these assumptions prove to be true, and it is indeed safe to be with others. A child has an unwritten contract with his or her parents, couples have written or unwritten contracts between each other, and people in general follow social rules as an unwritten contract. When this contract is broken, then the person can no longer assume it is safe. Take the example of the contract between a parent and a child:

   Parent <————————> Child

   Clearly this is not a written contract. After the birth of a child, a lawyer does not draw up a contract of safety between parent and child. However, if we were to write such a contract, what does the parent need to provide her children? (List on the board.)

Parental provision	Child's part
security	grow
safety	be a child
financial and emotional support	love
understanding	
unconditional love	
trust esteem	
hope	
guidance	

Similarly, contracts exist between husband and wife, teacher and student, police and citizen.

If your parent abused you, then he or she did not keep the contract. The parent was no longer able to provide for the child's needs. Every child needs the parent to keep the contract so she can grow and develop into a well-adjusted adult. However when this contract is broken as a result of the abuse, the child is shortchanged. You did not get what you deserved and what you needed. This experience is similar to domestic violence when the spouse becomes abusive and curtails the woman's capacity to grow and develop within the relationship as illustrated in Figure 5.5.

As you grow up, you no longer accept this basic contract among people: in fact, to protect yourself you assume it does not exist at all. The problem here is that to others, who still assume

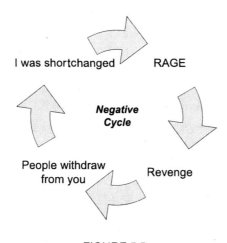

I was shortchanged   RAGE

Negative Cycle

People withdraw from you   Revenge

FIGURE 5.5.

it, it is as if *you* break the contract. They can tell that you do not uphold your side. You are the one viewed as paranoid, withholding, uptight, hostile, or critical. You become the one that cannot be trusted. So the cycle continues because you interpret all this as proof that others cannot be trusted. You end up creating a self-fulfilling prophecy of isolation and mistrust! The only way to break this prophecy is through forgiveness. What is forgiveness? It means "to give before." Before what? Before it is given. By this we mean that in your current relationships, when there is some kind of conflict, instead of concluding that the other person cannot be trusted, one needs to forgive the other for the problem in order to maintain the basic contract with them. To do this is to know the difference between what happened long ago, and the present. We do not mean forgiving the perpetrator, for usually his act is unforgivable. Let me illustrate how breaking the cycle helps to reestablish a sense of hope, support, safety, and esteem. (Redraw Figure 5.6 as an extension of the previous figure.)

3. Process Discussion
4. Wrap-Up

This negative cycle causes you to develop very rigid walls to protect yourself from the danger of the perpetrator. You had to build these walls for self-preservation. That was a good thing during the abuse. It helped you survive it. The problem is that

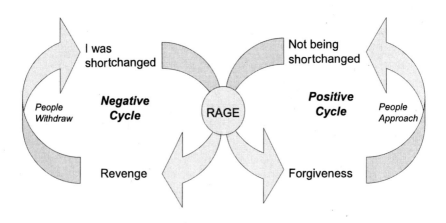

FIGURE 5.6.

you kept these walls even years after the danger was no longer present. You believed that you cannot trust others. You were filled up with revenge and mistrust of others, which led to your own isolation. In order to break this cycle, you have to acknowledge to yourself that you got a raw deal, which affected your entire life, a suffering that was unnecessary and probably unforgivable. Then you must attempt to reestablish and maintain the basic social contracts you have with other people now, by forgiving their small blunders and slights and put-downs, so that you can maintain connection with others who will support you. No one can avoid hurting you a little. It is important to separate the normal hurts in the present from the disastrous hurt of the trauma, and then to react differently.

5. Potential Challenges

"Am I supposed to forgive my perpetrator?"

Response: Some behaviors are not forgivable. You do not have to forgive the perpetrator. This is up to you. What we are talking about here is your capacity and readiness to forgive yourself. Many traumatized individuals blame the trauma on themselves and some of their self-destructive behavior may be an attempt to punish themselves. If you can remind yourself and accept that you were shortchanged, maybe you can forgive yourself.

"How do I know if it will be safe to trust someone?"

Response: It is hard to learn how and whom you can trust by isolating yourself from others. You have to have contact with people and take some chances to learn who is trustworthy. The more relationships you form, the more you learn about trust. You no longer can assume that people will not hurt you because someone who was supposed to protect you hurt you very badly. But not all people are there to hurt you. You must believe that.

SESSION 5: WOMANHOOD: MY ALLY OR MY ENEMY?

1. Main Points
   a. Women who were traumatized by another person often have a conflicted relationship with their gender identity.
   b. Traumatized women often attribute the pain of the trauma to the fact of being a woman.
   c. Womanhood and its associations are often viewed as the "enemy."
2. Minilecture

   Let's first define the words ally and enemy. I actually looked it up in the dictionary. What is your definition of ally and enemy? (List their answers on the board.)

Ally	Enemy
unite	inflict injury
friendly	unfriendly
helper	hostile

   Now, I want you to think of all the associations that you have with being a woman. Review in your mind your relationship to your gender (list their answers on the board; examples include: weakness, nurturing, dependency, body, sexual object, intimacy, sexual behavior, shame, betrayal, embarrassment, mothering, softness, submissiveness, etc.).

   Ask them to specify which associations they experience as ally or enemy. Circle the ones that they associate as enemy in the list that you just developed. Most often more of their associations to womanhood will be linked to "enemy." Now look back on the definition of enemy and reiterate how they view their gender as unfriendly or hostile. Point out how they tend to treat their gender as the enemy by hating it, hiding it, or injuring it. Ask them to list the ways that they have done this.

   • over- or undereating
   • promiscuity
   • substance abuse
   • self-defeating behaviors

3. Process Discussion
4. Wrap-Up

    During the abuse you experienced your womanhood as a source of pain, injury, and hostility. It is not surprising that you treat your gender as an enemy. It is not surprising that many women engage in self-destructive behaviors, as if they are dealing with an enemy. It is not your gender that betrayed you. Can you make peace with it?

5. Potential Challenges

    "My gender caused me more harm than good. Men still make comments on my appearance as a woman."

    Response: Raping and molestation have nothing to do with your gender. They have to do with the perpetrator's desire to exercise power over you. The perpetrator is able to control you not because of your gender but because of his position of power over you. Little boys are molested; in prison, the smaller men are molested. The perpetrator seeks a way to express his strength. Your helplessness during the trauma is not a sign of your being a woman but of your humanity. That is the core experience of trauma, profound helplessness, for both male and female victims.

    "Society treats women in a way that makes me hate my gender. There's nothing we can do about that!"

    Response: I can understand that. But it is still your responsibility to treat your womanhood well. Even more so. Sexualizing women the way our culture does, does not excuse the perpetrator. The perpetrator is responsible and accountable for the perpetration, not your gender.

Chapter 6

Phase II Sessions

SESSION 6: YOU ARE NOT THE TRAUMA

1. Main Points
   a. The effects of trauma are felt throughout the life cycle.
   b. Traumatized individuals feel engulfed by their trauma.
   c. The experience of trauma functions as a lens through which traumatized individuals see the world.
   d. Changing the relationship between the trauma and the self is an essential part of healing.
2. Minilecture

   Hand out Phase II booklets and review the purpose of Phase II, which is to examine the secondary effects of trauma on relationships and protective behaviors. Then tell them you are going to go through the stages of development from childhood to adulthood and look at the various effects of abuse. Name it the "Ripples of Abuse," and then redraw Figure 6.1.

   I would like to review with you some of the effects of trauma. Each age poses unique challenges for the developing person. Those of you who have children can attest to the vulnerability of the growing child. Abuse and mistreatment interfere with the child's ability to accomplish each developmental task, leaving her with negative feelings on the one hand, and increasingly maladaptive behaviors, on the other.

   As you can see, every stage of development is challenged by the detrimental consequences of the abuse. As time goes on, these effects slowly spread out into more and more areas of one's life, affecting things such as relationships and the ability to work. Many feel that they view themselves, others and the

Trauma-Centered Group Psychotherapy for Women
© 2008 by The Haworth Press, Taylor & Francis Group. All rights reserved.
doi:10.1300/6097_06

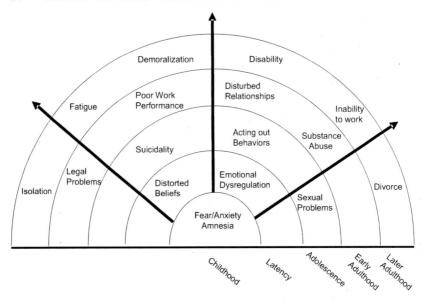

Figure 6.1.

world around them as if through the lens of the trauma. The traumatic experience infiltrates all their senses. They hear, see, and feel trauma. They are totally engulfed by the experience, becoming seized by it. Does that sound familiar? Recovery is about reversing this relationship, so that your traumatic experience remains as only one small part of who you are. (Redraw Figure 6.2 to demonstrate this relationship.)

3. Process Discussion
4. Wrap-Up

You can see how overwhelming the effects of the trauma on the self are. Often traumatized individuals feel engulfed by the trauma, as if it were a lens through which they see the world. In essence the self becomes embedded in the trauma. Your feelings, thoughts, and behavior are influenced by the traumatic experience. You as an individual become a small fraction of your day to day experience. Many of your decisions are based on your view of the world as distorted by the trauma. So you do not exist independently. What the perpetrator wanted seems to be continuing. We cannot change the past and take away the

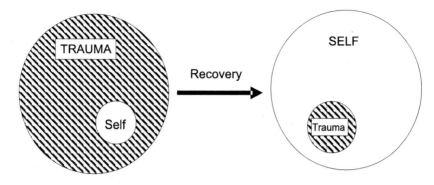

Figure 6.2.

trauma; however, we can help you reverse the relationship between you and the trauma. This will liberate you for your present and future. Your past always will include your traumatic experience. It is part of your personal history, but it does not have to be all of your life.

5. Potential Challenges

"Part of who I am today has to do with the trauma, so how can I let go of who I am?"

Response: The task is not to forget your trauma and how it affected you. There is no question it has affected who you are today. The goal is to separate the trauma from your perception of your self and people around you. If the trauma is in charge then it is dangerous to be around people and you are not in control of your destiny. That was true during the trauma. Now that the danger is over, you can be safe with people and you can be in control of your life and your future. You can defend yourself when you need to. More of you can be available to deal with the consequences of the trauma.

SESSION 7: KNOWING YOUR SYMPTOMS INCREASES YOUR CONTROL

1. Main Points
   a. The aftermath of trauma may form a chronic condition that requires ongoing management of symptoms.

   b. Learning about your symptoms leads to better management of them and to a heightened sense of control.

   c. Running scared from the symptoms leads to chaos and to more symptoms.

2. Minilecture

(Review the difference between acute versus chronic symptoms. Use a medical analogy such as heart attack versus angina to illustrate your point.) Heart attack, like the original trauma, requires acute management. The patient is hospitalized until the condition becomes stabilized. The goal is to stop the pain and to minimize the damage to the heart muscle. Angina, on the other hand, requires ongoing management. The patient needs to take medications and needs to learn the early warning signs of the condition to prevent it from becoming an acute medical crisis. Unlike acute symptoms, chronic symptoms require constant attention. If you do not attend to your symptoms they take over. The more you avoid dealing with the symptoms, the more risk for chaos is introduced into your life. What are the ways that you deal with your symptoms? (Give them different examples of common symptoms, such as insomnia, anxiety, pain, fear of intimacy, etc.)

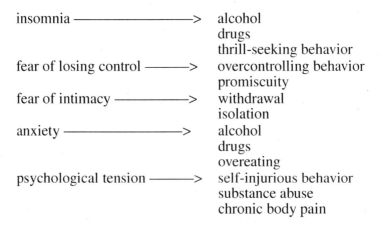

insomnia ————————>	alcohol
	drugs
	thrill-seeking behavior
fear of losing control ————>	overcontrolling behavior
	promiscuity
fear of intimacy ————————>	withdrawal
	isolation
anxiety ————————>	alcohol
	drugs
	overeating
psychological tension ————>	self-injurious behavior
	substance abuse
	chronic body pain

    The more you run scared from your symptoms, the more self-destructive your behavior becomes, the more chaos in your life, the more symptomatic you are! Let's take the example of flashbacks, which invade your mind from the past. Intrusive memo-

ries are not as bad. But by actively remembering your traumatic
events, you take control over your mind. (Recreate Figure 6.3 to
illustrate this point.)

Running from your symptoms creates a vicious cycle that fuels your symptoms and your despair. In fact, avoiding dealing
with the symptoms makes your condition worse. So what can
you do about it? Exactly! Break the cycle. How?
(List on the board:)

- Get sober
- Get clean of drugs
- Stop the running
- Manage your symptoms

3. Process Discussion
4. Wrap-Up

Remember the relationship between the Self and Trauma?
(Draw Figure 6.2 again.)

The more you know your symptoms, the more control you
have over them, the more control you have over YOU. You need
to learn to control your symptoms so they will not control you.

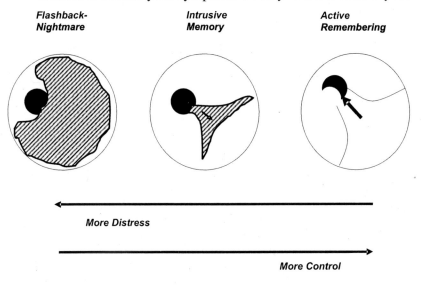

Figure 6.3.

- You need to talk about them
- Stop running scared from them
- Learn your triggers
- Manage your symptoms

5. Potential Challenges

"It is the lack of control that I experience that leads me to run away from my symptoms."

Response: The sense of not having control is one of the symptoms of your condition. Trauma causes the person to feel out of control, just like you were out of control during the traumatic event. Reminding yourself that this feeling is just a feeling from the past will help you to exercise control over the moment. Trying to "manage" this feeling with alcohol or food leads to out-of-control behavior, which becomes a self-defeating cycle.

"Sometimes even when I manage my symptoms they get worse. For example, my nightmares got worse when I stopped drinking."

Response: That is true. At the beginning your symptoms may worsen. But they will diminish in due time. What happened to your nightmares with the drinking over the years? Right, they got worse. Avoidance was no longer working. In fact avoidance made the nightmares worse, which is probably one of the reasons you decided to quit. With sobriety, the nightmares will get better over time. With alcohol they will get worse over time.

SESSION 8: YOUR BODY IS NOT YOUR ENEMY

1. Main Points
   a. During the traumatic event, the body experiences anxiety, fear, and pain.
   b. Because of these experiences, victims feel their body failed them or let them down.

    c. Experiencing the body as an enemy leads to self-destructive
      behaviors.
    d. Taking care of one's body is essential to the healing process.
2. Minilecture

We believe you treat your body as if it is your enemy. First, let's review how you treat an enemy. (Ask them.) Exactly. You do not trust it; you fear it, you hate it, and you want to kill it. Now try to remember what your body experienced during the trauma. (Ask them and list their responses on the board: paralysis, tension, weakness, terror, racing heart, sweatiness pain, anxiety, disconnection, etc.)

These are normal reactions human beings have in response to danger. Your mind and body assessed the situation during the trauma and moved into fight-or-flight responses. It is our instinct to do so for self-preservation. It is part of the fear response that helps us respond to danger. Those are physiological and automatic responses. You do not have control over them and that is a good thing, so your body can better prepare itself for survival. However, it is not surprising that you experience your body as the enemy since it expressed all the experiences that you attributed to the enemy, namely, fearing it, not trusting it, and hating it. During sexual abuse your body may have responded in the way it is wired to respond with stimulation. This experience is particularly confusing because the woman may then question her participation in the abuse. Women often feel guilty about it and embarrassed by it. That is understandable but it has nothing to do with your choices. It has to do with physiological responses. So how did you *kill* these sensations? (Ask them and list them on the board.)

- alcohol and drugs
- self-destructive behaviors
- thrill-seeking behavior
- abuse/mutilation
- neglect of health
- promiscuity

3. Process Discussion

4. Wrap-Up

It is understandable how you react to your body. However your body responded to the abuse, your body is not the abuse itself. The associations you listed represent the trauma, not your body. Therefore you have to (list on the board):

- Take care of your body
- Read it correctly; assess if danger is really present
- Soothe it
- Work with it
- Treat it like an ally, not an enemy

5. Potential Challenges

"I hated the abuse by my father, but he also treated me well at other times."

Response: It is very confusing to have a parent who at times can be caring and other times hurtful. Your challenge is to find a way to have those conflicted feelings coexist. You can love your parent and still hold him accountable for his actions.

"I hated the abuse but there were parts that I enjoyed, which makes me feel so bad and disgusted."

Response: Your body is wired to respond to stimulation and it may feel pleasurable. That does not mean that you participated in the abuse or enjoyed it. If you were in any position to control the situation, what would you have done? Exactly! Stopped it. But you were not in charge or in control. That is the nature of trauma. The perpetrator is in charge, not the victim.

SESSION 9: CUTTING OFF PEOPLE CONTINUES YOUR ISOLATION

1. Main Points

a. The moment of trauma is characterized by an overwhelming sense of isolation.

   b. Cutting off others in the service of survival is an adaptive-coping strategy.
   c. Continuing to cut off people after the trauma interferes with healing.
2. Minilecture

   At the moment of trauma a lot is cut off: part of the self, other people, and the environment. Traumatized individuals often report amnesia for parts of the event, or that they feel as if it happened to somebody else. We call this cutting off process, *dissociation*. Dissociation helps the person survive the horrific moment of the trauma. Even if the trauma occurs with other people present (e.g., war, natural disaster), the experience of the traumatic moment is of being all alone. Other people are cut off from your experience. At the moment of the trauma, the sole priority is survival and therefore cutting off everything for this purpose is adaptive. This defense mechanism helps us survive. However, when danger is no longer present, it becomes maladaptive to continue to utilize the same defense mechanism of cutting off. By constantly removing oneself from connections to others, you end up alone, over and over again. Let's list some of the people whom you have cut off. (Redraw Figure 6.4 to illustrate this point.)

   Have group members mention who they cut off and represent it by a line crossing the circle, which represents the self (see Figure 6.5). They often mention spouse, lover, siblings, parents, children, boss, coworkers, friends, and therapists. After you list all the people they cut off, ask them what happened as a result. Yes, they are all alone again. To illustrate your point even more strongly, ask them what type of person is usually cut off from everybody.) Right, a prisoner. (Draw the circle again in Figure 6.5; this time with prison bars.) You become a prisoner of your own defenses.
3. Process Discussion
4. Wrap-Up

   What started as an adaptive defense mechanism ended up increasing your suffering. It is like an allergic response. The body wants to protect you but overdoes it. For example, an asthma attack is the body's attempt to protect you from whatever you are allergic to. When this happens you feel quite ill and in severe

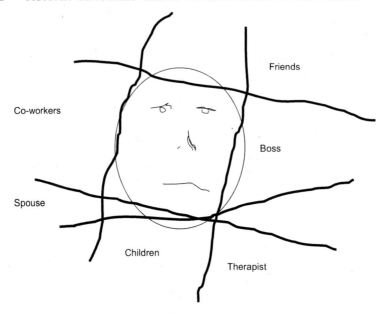

Figure 6.4.

conditions, you even die. In our example, the asthma response is analogous to cutting people off (your response). The severe symptoms of asthma (shortness of breath) are analogous to your isolation. You were all alone during the traumatic moment and you are all alone now. You became a prisoner of your defense mechanisms. So what can you do about it?

- Be aware of it
- Let others know when you cut them off
- Try again

5. Potential Challenges

"I am aware of my isolation but I feel safer this way."

Response: I know that you feel safe in your isolation. But what motivated this behavior? Yes, the fear of being hurt. You were hurt badly during your abuse. But not everyone is going to hurt

Figure 6.5.

you. You have to remember that the fears are part of your past and not necessarily part of the present. Assess if there is danger. If there is none then try to let someone in. Perhaps you will discover that this experience may make you feel safe as well.

"Being alone is not a bad thing. I love it."

Response: Being alone is a good thing. Being lonely and isolated is not. If you really make a free choice to be alone, then, fine. However, if you stay isolated out of fear of being hurt again, then you have allowed the trauma to continue to control your life. The perpetrator is in charge again, even though he/she is long gone.

SESSION 10: STOP THE DUMPING

1. Main Points
   a. The experience of trauma can be described as dumping by the perpetrator, bystander, and society.

b. As a result of this dumping, the victim learns to utilize dump-ing when she experiences real or perceived danger.

c. Using dumping as a defense mechanism interferes with re-covery.

2. Minilecture

What is dumping? Right! Dumping is unloading or throwing away rubbish. You have been dumped on during the abuse or your traumatic event. Who dumped on you? (Recreate Figure 6.6 to illustrate your example.)

Have them mention the people who they experienced as dumpers: perpetrators, bystanders, collaborators, authority fig-ures, family members, etc. You have been dumped on by many people. Over the years the container has been filled up with rub-bish. (Illustrate different layers of the container representing the "rubbish": shame, humiliation, poor esteem, self-hatred, incom-petence, inadequacies, feeling dirty, etc.) Now I am going to use an analogy to make the point. What is the place in the house where we dump particularly disgusting stuff? Yes, the toilet.

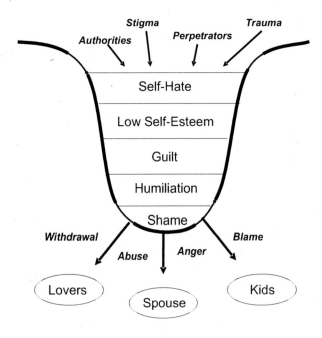

Figure 6.6.

When it fills up you need to flush it in order to keep it clean and functional. What will happen if you do not flush it? Right, it will spill out all over. What a mess. When you get filled up with the rubbish you also need to flush it. If you do not, you feel like bursting. It is like emotional plumbing. How do you flush out these ugly feelings? (List on the drawing: anger outburst, yelling, putting down, withdrawal, etc.) On whom do you flush? (List the people they mention: spouse, kids, lovers, siblings, friends, co-workers, etc.) Exactly! You dump on the people who are close to you, even though they are not your perpetrator. What do these people do when you have dumped on them? Yes, move away from you, and bingo, you are left alone again. But this time it is because of an action you have taken.

3. Process Discussion
4. Wrap-Up

You were dumped on, which made you feel resentful, leading to you dumping on others. They then feel resentful and they dump back on you or withdraw from you. The sad part is that what the perpetrator did to you continues, long after the perpetrator is gone. A vicious cycle is created. The perpetrator gets off scot-free, while your relationships with loved ones are ruined. (See Figure 6.7 and redraw to illustrate this point.)

You need to break this cycle:

Be aware of your need to dump out bad feelings.

Apologize when you dump on others.

Recognize when you're dumped on and by whom.

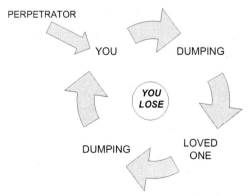

Figure 6.7.

5. Potential Challenges

"I usually dump after I was dumped on. I don't initiate this behavior."

Response: This vicious cycle needs to end and the only way
to end it is by breaking it. Someone has to start and it may as
well be you. Exercise control over your life and your relationships.

"I have been in this vicious cycle for a long time and I apolo-
gized for it numerous times. I think it is too late."

Response: Maybe it is too late. But did you ever talk to your
family about your trauma? Did you ever explain to them where
this behavior is coming from? Now that you understand it better,
maybe you can help them understand it. Is it worth trying?

SESSION 11: PUTTING IT RIGHT

1. Main Points
   a. The victim was wronged by the perpetrator, which heightened
      the victim's sensitivity to injustice and unfairness.
   b. It is human nature to seek justice.
   c. An exaggerated attempt to seek justice by the victim reflects
      her wish to have been treated fairly by the perpetrator.
2. Minilecture
   When you were wronged by the perpetrator you were not
   able to put it right. You were out of control and powerless. That
   is the experience of trauma. As a result of that experience, you
   developed an acute sensitivity to injustice and unfairness. As an
   adult, when you detect anything wrong or unjust you are often
   propelled to set it right. How many of you find yourself as the
   person who speaks up for the group at work or other settings?
   Get involved in lawsuits? Have problems with authority? You
   feel that you have to do it. It almost feels that you have no
   choice. You try to get justice for yourself in every place but the
   original place, so you can never be satisfied. (Make a list of the

examples given by group members of the situations when they felt compelled to set something right.)

However, this does not make you feel better and often leads to problems. One example is that people who are unburdened by trauma are usually willing, in the end, to compromise. But for you, any compromise, no matter how small, is unacceptable, because that means defeat, again. You never let go, and people feel you are impossible to deal with.

So what is the problem? The problem is that your effort in putting things right reflects your initial hope that justice would have been done and you would have not been wronged. But that did not happen. Part of your burden is to know that you were wronged and that it was not right, and there is probably nothing that you can do about the past. If there is something you can do about the original event, then that is what you should do.

3. Process Discussion
4. Wrap-Up

By stopping the displacement and by acknowledging you were wronged, you restore more control and balance into your life. Knowing that you were wronged by the perpetrator, knowing that justice was not served, is knowing about suffering and trauma. God knows you know all about that. The way to restore justice is for you to become aware of other people's suffering and to appreciate their struggle. We appreciate yours!

5. Potential Challenges

"I am tired of being the one who does the work. I suffered as a child and now I am suffering as an adult. When is it going to end?"

Response: You are describing the existential experience of the traumatized person. You are the one who needs to carry the burden and work so hard. It is not fair but that is the way it is. This time though, you can be the one in control and make choices for yourself. In this way, you can defeat the trauma.

Chapter 7

Phase III Sessions

SESSION 12: FINDING MEANING IN YOUR LIFE

1. Main Points
   a. The trauma is meaningless; it is the process of recovery that generates meaning.
   b. Giving testimony often helps to discover new meaning, and transcend the traumatic experience.
   c. Healing from trauma must happen within a social context.
2. Minilecture

   Hand out Phase III booklets, and review Phase III, which will be about meaning, mourning, and testimony, with the group. Remind them of the upcoming ceremony and find out who they are planning to bring in as witnesses. Find out who they asked already and who are they planning to ask. Encourage them to do it now and not at the last moment. Underscore the importance of the ceremony. You most likely will meet with resistance and fear. You can underscore how important this event is for their healing. Make a reference to the ceremony each week from now on, and connect it to each of the thematic lectures.

   In order to heal, you need to transcend the traumatic experience. The trauma is not meaningful in itself, for we describe it as a senseless act. But humans believe that things have meaning, so usually the victim comes to the conclusion that the horrible event occurred to them because they somehow deserved it. When lightning strikes a house on our street and burns it to the ground, a random act, everyone thinks, "Oh, that makes sense," for we can all think of reasons why someone does not match the ideal.

Trauma-Centered Group Psychotherapy for Women
© 2008 by The Haworth Press, Taylor & Francis Group. All rights reserved.
doi:10.1300/6097_07

True meaning, however, can be created through the recovery process. One of the most powerful ways of discovering the meaning of your trauma is to simply tell your story to someone else, and then listen to them. They will tell you the real meaning of the traumatic event, and you will be surprised by what they will say. Of course you will not be invited to tell your story. Your first act of courage is to ignore the voices that wish to silence you, and speak. The perpetrator told you not to speak, your family probably indicated they would be too upset if you spoke, and society indicated that it wouldn't believe you, since what happened was unbelievable. But the story of your suffering must come out. You will learn that many people have suffered traumatic experiences similar to yours. You will be able to receive support from some. You will educate others. You will give strength to other victims who are strangled by fear. What could be more meaningful than this? In so doing, you transform a meaningless act of perpetration into a meaningful act of restoration and strength.

Testimony requires (1) someone to tell the story—the trauma survivor, and (2) someone to listen to it—the witness.

The moment of trauma is a deathless void, all connection with others is gone. So it makes sense that the process of recovery must take place in connection with another, the story now re-told in the presence of a caring witness. If only that witness had seen what happened! But he or she will see and feel what happened as you tell it, and die with you, and survive with you. It is the presence of the witness that allows your suffering to be mourned, your strength to survive honored.

3. Process Discussion
4. Wrap-Up

In order to transcend the trauma you have to give testimony of your experience. You need to learn to share the burden by letting others know about your ordeal. By sharing this burden you will allow someone to support you. No one can understand what you have been through without your educating them about the trauma and its aftermath. It is your obligation to educate us and it is our responsibility to listen to you. So what are the ways to find meaning in your life? (List on the board.)

- Tell your story
- Educate
- Help other victims
- Allow yourself to get support

5. Potential Challenges

"So much of who I am today is a result of my trauma. I don't feel it was meaningless."

Response: The trauma itself is meaningless. What meaning is there in beating or demeaning a child? What meaning is there in raping a woman? No meaning at all. What is meaningful is what you have done in your pursuit of life, despite this. What is meaningful is your attempt to make people understand what happened even though it is incomprehensible.

SESSION 13: MOVING INTO THE FUTURE

1. Main Points
   a. Moving into the future requires a good understanding of the past.
   b. Maladaptive coping skills (e.g., isolation) and cognitive distortions (e.g., "no one can understand me") hinder the capacity to move on.
   c. By breaking the silence, by improving communication, and by developing support networks, victims can become survivors.
2. Minilecture
   What stands in the way of your future? (Ask them and list on the board.)

- isolation
- disconnection
- confusion
- mistrust of others

These are all examples of symptoms and experiences of the trauma, of the past. The past keeps you imprisoned with the trauma. As long as the trauma keeps a hold on you, the more symptomatic you will become. In order for you to move on, you need to:

- Break the silence
- Improve communication
- Widen your support network
- Help others

We cannot change the past or take away the trauma. It is part of your past history. However, you can be in control of your future and determine what direction it will take. The more you engage in the present and the future, the more you will gain control over your life. You will win, the trauma will lose.

3. Process Discussion
4. Wrap-Up

In order to move into the future, you need to respect and know the past. Know the trauma since its voices are strong and want to remain in control over you. The more you empower yourself by letting others know about it and receiving support, the stronger you will be. How can you make your voice heard? (Ask them and list on the board.)

- Talk, tell, communicate
- Let others support you
- Empower other voices

5. Potential Challenges

"Letting people know about my past may cause them to leave me."

Response: Anyone who would leave because they learned of your suffering, you can spare. Would you leave anyone who suffers as much as you? Give your family or friends the credit they deserve. Try them. You can decide on the pace or amount of disclosure. You can be in control of that. If they let you down, find others who will really be there for you.

SESSION 14: SAYING GOODBYE

1. Main Points
   a. Saying goodbye may remind you of the losses suffered during the trauma.
   b. Traumatized individuals avoid saying goodbye, fearing they will reexperience the trauma.
   c. Learning to differentiate between mourning the trauma and saying goodbye is essential for recovery.
2. Minilecture
    The group is about to end and therefore saying goodbye to one another is very important. Let us explore the difficulty you may experience in saying goodbye and examine its connection to the trauma. What associations do you have with saying goodbye? (List on the board.)

   - loss
   - death
   - fear
   - abandonment
   - rejection
   - ending/finality
   - anxiety
   - transition
   - beginning

   If you look at the list, almost every item could also describe the trauma. Therefore, it is not surprising that people who were traumatized will avoid saying goodbye or will experience overwhelming anxiety when saying it. Trauma is all about loss and therefore it evokes much pain and anxiety. It is important to realize that your response to "goodbye" is linked to your experience of the trauma. The pain and fear that you experience in anticipating goodbye is directly linked to the trauma. Saying goodbye is not by itself harmful. It may represent loss but it is not traumatic. Acknowledging an end or a loss is a necessary step in moving on to new things and relationships. Life is change. It is only when change is sudden, unexpected, painful, and out of your control, that it is traumatic. Saying goodbye is burdened when the loss experienced during the trauma has not been fully mourned. When a death occurs, we mourn, and it is proper to mourn the death of the person you were before the trauma. Mourn. Mourning calls out for a shoulder to catch your tears, mourning offers a hand to squeeze. Yet no goodbye today can be as painful as your trauma.

3. Process Discussion

4. Wrap-Up

Every time you need to say goodbye the past will intrude. When it surfaces you need to:

- Identify its connection to the trauma
- Assess if real danger exists
- Reassure yourself
- Accept support

Every goodbye now is actually a blessing, for you should be able to remind yourself that it is not the traumatic loss. Every goodbye now is another opportunity to quietly mourn that past self whom you lost long ago. Now and then are different. Now is a much safer place.

5. Potential Challenges

"I never say goodbye no matter what. I always say see you later."

Response: Do you know why you never say goodbye? Right. You are afraid that the feeling from the past when you were traumatized will surface and you will reexperience the pain. By avoiding dealing with loss you paradoxically keep yourself closer to the trauma, leading to continued pain. You are checkmated. Try dealing with it and you may find out that the pain will slowly diminish.

"Saying goodbye is too final."

Response: Saying goodbye acknowledges the end or the loss. By making closure, a goodbye opens the possibilities for new beginning. The origin of the sense of finality is the darkness surrounding the trauma.

SESSION 15: ACHIEVING TRANSFORMATION

1. Main Points
   a. The process of healing is comprised of numerous transformations.
   b. Healing ceremonies provide a setting for transformations to occur.
2. Minilecture

   The process of healing involves many transformations. Healing ceremonies like the one we are going to have at the end of our program offer an opportunity for these transformations to take place. Let us review the different transformations that are part of the healing process:

   isolation ————————> sharing
   silence ————————> expression
   shame/self-blame ————————> pride
   demoralization ————————> hope
   passivity ————————> educator
   emptiness ————————> meaning

   Each of the transformations, which we have been working on in this group, is going to be symbolized during the ceremony.

   - sharing in a public setting
   - breaking the silence through your testimony
   - transcendence through creativity
   - generation of hope
   - active role as an educator
   - generation of meaning

   We are all going to take part in the transformation: You—by giving testimony and educating people about recovery from trauma; the witnesses—by honoring your story and validating your experience; the audience—by taking responsibility for society. Together we will work on defeating the voices of despair. Together we will fight against the trauma. You will no longer need to be alone in this struggle.
3. Process Discussion

4. Wrap-Up

The process of healing involves many transformations that are the culmination of many rehearsals for change throughout your life. The ceremony is one metaphor for transformation of suffering into healing. By breaking the silence you build connections and by sharing the burden you shatter your isolation. The more you keep the secret of the past, the more you empower the trauma to keep you hostage. The more you share your burden with others, the more you will mourn, and it is through mourning that darkness finds light. You are no longer alone! It is no longer night.

5. Potential Challenges

"I never told anyone of my trauma. How can I do it in the presence of strangers?"

Response: The more you keep your story secret, the more you protect the perpetrator and his power over you. The perpetrator told you not to tell for a reason. The more isolated you become from the support of others, the more vulnerable you are to the trauma. Even though your perpetrator may no longer be around, the spell of his power is ever present. By breaking the silence you are breaking this spell.

"I cannot disclose my trauma publicly. It is too difficult."

Response: You can disclose as much as you feel comfortable with or as much as you are ready to. Your testimony should represent your journey of healing. Many women choose to disclose their traumas but you don't have to. You are in charge of this decision. We will honor it.

"I don't have anyone who can function as my witness."

Response: Your isolation really cut you off from everyone. Let's review those who are currently in your life (mention all family members, friends, co-workers, therapists, clergy). Is there anyone who really cares to listen? Is there anyone who is genuinely interested in your welfare? If the answer is no, then we need to work harder on widening your support network. You should come to the ceremony and we will assign a witness for you from the audience (no group member or group therapist can be a witness). If the answer is yes, then this is your witness!

SESSION 16: STANDING IN THE TRUTH OF ONE'S TESTIMONY

In this meeting, each group member presents her testimony to the group. This piece can be in the form of narrative, poem, art project, music, etc. Later they will present these in the public ceremony where family members, friends, therapists, or people from their support network will function as witnesses. In the intimate setting of the group, the group serves as the witnesses and responds to each one of them. These spontaneous exchanges are very powerful and tend to be quite emotional. Some will bring a small souvenir to each member as a goodbye gift. The group meeting ends with the therapists' reflections on each member's progress during the treatment. At the very end the group leader stands up and presents to each member a certificate of graduation. One by one a group member will stand up to get her certificate as the rest applaud. The group members then leave the group space and the therapists set up the room for the ceremony. The group members and their witnesses will gather in the room later for the ceremony.

Chapter 8

The Graduation Ceremony

The graduation ceremony has been included in the TCGP model due to its ability to enhance the therapeutic effects of the group experience, and to solidify members' commitment to changing their behavior after the group ends. Our ceremony is based on previous work with traumatized populations, which the reader may wish to consult for greater details (Johnson, Feldman, Lubin, & Southwick, 1995; Lubin & Johnson, 1998; Lubin & Johnson, 2003).

Healing ceremonies, through their use of formalization and dramatization, confer upon the participants the feeling that what is occurring has broader significance to the society at large (Lubin & Johnson, 1998). At the heart of the ceremony is a symbolic transformation, in which the participants pass from one state to another, overcoming certain symbolic obstacles, fears, or tests (Johnson, 1987). In therapeutic ceremonies, this transformation represents the achievement of improved relationships among members. Framed within the ceremonial space, such transformations are afforded the implicit or explicit approval of the "congregation" or the larger society. Thus ceremonies help to recontextualize the experience of trauma victims, giving meaning to their alienation (Silver & Wilson, 1988). The fundamental break in relationship between them and society can then be addressed.

We will now briefly describe the essential therapeutic functions of the graduation ceremony: (1) giving testimony and bearing witness, (2) inviting society to take on responsibility for its members, and (3) providing a positive homecoming experience.

Trauma-Centered Group Psychotherapy for Women
© 2008 by The Haworth Press, Taylor & Francis Group. All rights reserved.
doi:10.1300/6097_08

89

GIVING TESTIMONY AND BEARING WITNESS

The ceremony provides the trauma survivor with an opportunity to tell the audience of her ordeal. Clients are told to prepare a testimony that reflects their journey of recovery. The testimony can be an expression in any medium that the client chooses, such as writing, visual art, or music. This task generates anxiety in these women, for it extends the act of revelation to a much wider arena. Nevertheless, in our experience, each participant has elected to disclose her traumatic event during the ceremony.

Many of the women who have participated in the program had rarely disclosed their traumatic events. Many felt it was their duty to keep it secret in order to protect their loved ones, or as a reflection of their self-blame and shame regarding the experience. It is hoped that they learn in the program that their silence protects the perpetrator, that bearing witness brings shame upon the evil-doer, not the victim. Standing up publicly and "coming out" is a terrifying, and liberating, experience. The woman's silent pain is transformed into an audible voice. Her private knowledge of the traumatic experience is transformed into public acknowledgement of her suffering. Her painful isolation is transformed into visible connection and communication. Through these transformations, the victim embraces an active stance over her traumatic story, and gains mastery over the fears that have sustained her passivity previously. A number of clients have become mobilized into activist roles as victim advocates, aiming to educate society and empower other victims to move toward recovery and healing. The majority of clients, however, have simply gained greater empowerment within their own families. Case 8.1 illustrates this process.

Case 8.1: Laura

Laura is thirty years old. She was neglected by her parents and as a result looked up to her older brother to be her protector and role model. When she was eight years old her brother sexually assaulted and humiliated her in front of his friends. She shut down completely, never told anyone about the abuse, and was convinced that it was her fault and that she deserved it. Her distress and her pain surfaced in disguised forms: depression, eating disorder, and multiple suicide attempts. Despite numerous treatment settings she did not reveal her past and held firmly to the belief that she failed in keeping her brother's love. In the last year and a half she was able to connect with a therapist whom she trusts, and revealed some aspects of her trauma. She was referred to the Women's Trauma Program to address her trauma in a group setting.

Laura was a very compliant group member. She was able to tell the group about her traumatic experience, however she held strongly to her belief that it was her fault and that she must have done something bad to deserve it. Despite numerous efforts by group members to point out to her that she did not deserve to be treated this way and that her brother betrayed her trust, Laura was not able to shift her view. She told the group that her husband had tried to convince her but she did not believe he was being truthful. After all, she was a source of a lot of distress in their marriage with several hospitalizations and numerous suicide attempts, the most recent one almost claiming her life. Over the course of the group, however, she became less resistant to feedback and support from the group and on several occasions even admitted to having thoughts that she might not be to blame. In preparation for the ceremony, Laura expressed her anxiety but also expressed commitment to participate in it. Significantly, she invited her husband to serve as her witness. At the ceremony Laura read the following testimony, which she named "My Testimony."

- "These are words that I haven't been able to say, or believe, until now: It wasn't my fault."
- "I was just a little girl. I was seeking love, acceptance, and approval. I trusted my brother, and that wasn't wrong. But what happened to me was very wrong. He betrayed that trust. My brother and his friends sexually assaulted me when I was eight years old. And though I've carried a tremendous amount of shame over many years, and I blamed myself for what they did to me, and for trusting them, it was not my fault."
- "When I was raped by a boyfriend at age fifteen, I blamed myself for that, too. But that wasn't my fault. I trusted him and he took advantage of that trust and hurt me. The shame that I feel for these traumas doesn't belong to me and so I am giving it back to you who have hurt me. My pain and sadness almost cost me my life. And it's hard for me to learn about the traumas underneath the pain and sadness. I want so much to move beyond the pain and find happiness and feel life differently. To feel life not as a painful experience that must be endured, but as a rich experience filled with happiness, joy, love, and even sorrow, pain, and sadness."
- "I feel as though I am at the beginning of a journey in my recovery process. I am only starting to accept the reality of the traumas in my life. Accept them as part of my history. I am just learning about my own pain. It is powerful and mighty, but not stronger than me. I am only beginning to discover the anger I feel toward those who hurt me. Anger that I had turned on myself. I am just learning that, despite the immense shame and guilt that I feel, what happened to me was not my fault."

Jim, Laura's husband, with tears in his eyes, responded to her, "You are right, Laura. It was not your fault, and now both of us are going to fight it together. I love you and am very proud of you." The couple reached for each other and hugged each other for a long while. When they finished, a member of the audience stood up and said loudly, "Laura, it was not your fault." And then the entire audience stood and said those important words to Laura.

INVITING SOCIETY TO TAKE ON RESPONSIBILITY FOR ITS MEMBERS

Even though the experience of trauma is an isolating and lonely one, the process of healing is best accomplished in a social context. The audience serves as witnesses to the victim's testimony, and they provide a healing, positive welcome home. But beyond these important functions, the participation of the audience in the graduation ceremony serves to underscore the responsibility that society must take on for its victimized members, and the commitment to address the conditions that lead to such assaults on its members. Thus the audience's role is not merely to be witnesses and communicate sympathy, but to share the burden of stopping crime, sexual abuse, and rape. As individual women air their stories, their burden should in some way be lifted; the audience on the other hand should be weighed down by the increased awareness of the tragic events occurring all around them. Case 8.2 illustrates the importance of the family taking responsibility and sharing the burden.

Case 8.2: Kim

Kim had a very enmeshed and difficult relationship with her mother, whom she experienced as unsupportive and aloof. In her early teens she experienced the tragic death of her young brother, the premature death of her father (who was an alcoholic but not abusive), and the death of her grandfather (who was the most supportive and nurturing figure in her life). Kim felt that her mother was disappointed that she (Kim) was not the one who died. Her mother had treated her with a cold, formal contempt. In her early twenties, Kim was brutally raped at knife point, and then thrown out of the rapist's car. She became pregnant from the rape, and decided to carry it to term, which enraged her mother. The mother refused to have anything to do with Kim's child.

The focus of Kim's treatment was on disentangling the relationship between her mother and the rape. She struggled against replaying her relationship with her mother by being emotionally distant from her own daughter, who was a constant reminder of the perpetrator. However, in the graduation ceremony, Kim unveiled a series of beautiful pictures depicting the way she felt about herself, her daughter, and the mother she had always wished she had. As her mother witnessed her daughter's graduation, Kim described the events symbolized in her paintings, including her mother's emotional neglect. Kim began crying and was able for the first time to tell her mother how she felt unloved by her and how much she needed her support. Her mother, attempting to maintain control but obviously very moved, publicly told Kim how much she loved her and how proud she was to see her fight her devastating past. She then said she realized that Kim had had to fight it alone, because she had been too concerned about her own welfare to be able to care for her daughter. Bursting into tears, the mother asked for Kim's forgiveness for these shortcomings, saying that there was no longer any need for them to feel so alone. This display of taking responsibility was of profound help to Kim in her process of recovery.

PROVIDING A POSITIVE HOMECOMING EXPERIENCE

Often after the traumatic event the victim experiences a real or perceived rejection by her support system and society. She may experience society as blaming of, insensitive to, or intolerant of her, while excusing or even protecting her perpetrator. The experience of negative homecoming contributes to the isolation and estrangement of the victim, which may lead to greater symptom formation (Johnson et al., 1997). Societal attitudes toward female sexual assault victims as exaggerating, manipulating, or stuck in the past are not uncommon. Despite the fact that the audience at the graduation ceremony obviously consists of people supportive of the women, the women very often experience real fear that their testimonies will be scorned, ignored, or rejected. The audience, as representatives of society at large, can thus offer the women a positive homecoming experience through their presence, respect, and support. The ceremony highlights this encounter between victim and society, allowing for profound desensitizing effects on the women's fears of revealing their traumatic experience. A powerful homecoming is reflected in Case 8.3

Case 8.3: Sue

Sue was gang-raped when she was nineteen years old. The crime was reported to the police and the gang members were brought to trial. As a child she had been molested by her alcoholic father. Her mother had been a passive bystander who had not intervened even though she knew what was happening. After the gang rape her parents did not provide support and blamed her for it. In fact, several weeks after the gang rape, Sue's father raped her, telling her if other men could have her, he could too. For the next twenty-five years Sue ran away from her memories and her fears. She was completely isolated and used drugs and alcohol to ease the pain. During the previous year she had attained sobriety and begun treatment in the Women's Trauma Program, which was her first group experience. For the graduation ceremony she invited her husband to be her witness.

(Sue's husband is asked to stand on the other side of the room from the women.)

Maintaining distance between the client and her family members is an important symbolic indicator of the chasm that separates them, and over which they must pass during the ceremony, and in their lives.

LEADER: We came here today to break the silence and to listen to the untold. Are those gathered here willing to witness the stories of these women?

EVERYONE: Yes we are!

Again, beginning the ceremony with a statement of commitment by the societal witnesses places the individual transformation of the clients into a larger context, as well as providing them a sense of legitimacy that many had not received.

LEADER: Sue, have you suffered a traumatic event as a child or as an adult?

SUE: Yes, I have.

LEADER: When you experienced your trauma did you feel terror, pain, or overwhelming fear?

SUE: Yes, I did.

LEADER: That is trauma.

EVERYONE: That is trauma.

LEADER: As a result of the trauma, did you experience shame, guilt, or self-doubt?

SUE: Very much so.

LEADER: You are not to blame.

EVERYONE: You are not to blame.

The client is in a vulnerable, sensitized state, filled with her traumatic schema; the repetition of these basic, normative statements is designed to interfere with these traumatic voices.

LEADER: After the traumatic experience, were you put down, stigmatized, betrayed or rejected?

SUE: (tearfully) I was humiliated.

LEADER: You were let down.

EVERYONE: You were let down.

LEADER: Did you feel confused, shut down, or isolated?

SUE: I lost my mind and my life.

LEADER: We are here for you tonight.

EVERYONE: We are here for you tonight.

LEADER: As a result of your pain and the trauma did you cut off people that you love?

SUE: (tearfully looking at her husband across the room) Yes.

LEADER: Lose control of your anger and hurt people that you love?

SUE: Yes.

LEADER: Felt so numb that hurting yourself was the only thing to do?

SUE: Yes I cut myself many times.

LEADER: Did you resort to drugs or alcohol to silence the pain?

SUE: Yes.

LEADER: Did you think of suicide as a way of ending it all?

SUE: I tried to kill myself.

Despite the obvious sympathy and support offered the client, identifying her own responsibility for her maladaptive coping behaviors is essential to provide balance, as well as establish a basis for empathy with suffering family members.

LEADER: Is there still hope?

SUE: (pauses and looks at the Leader) Yes.

LEADER: Yes we believe there is hope.

EVERYONE: Yes we believe there is hope.

LEADER: Did you have experiences that kept you and your story silent?

SUE: No one wanted to listen to me.

LEADER: We are listening now.

EVERYONE: We are listening now.

LEADER: Tell us about your struggle.

This is the "test" or passage that the client and her family are asked to make in this ceremony, for giving public testimony is to forsake the injunction of the perpetrator to forever remain silent; for listening to this testimony with tolerance, family members must give up their denial and shame. Once through this breach, their relationship to the trauma is transformed.

Sue stepped forward with a stick covered with different color strands. "In keeping with the Mohawk tradition I made this talking stick. The wood is white birch with the bark removed. I painted it flat black to represent my life, my self. The tip of the talking stick I painted white for truth. This band of yellow represents my friend. I witnessed his suicide. The red stripes symbolize the motorcycle gang that tied, tortured, and raped me over Easter weekend twenty-five years ago. The black color strands between the red symbolize my father molesting me from age two, culminating in a rape just weeks after I was gang-raped. The gray color stands for my mother who allowed the years of sexual abuse from my father to continue, who enabled his alcoholism, blames me for getting raped, who lives in denial and will not validate any of my memories. The blue color symbolizes my coping methods of rage, alcoholism, drug abuse, cigarettes, and isolation. The bottom of this talking stick is a deer hoof to symbolize the times I might have escaped if the gang had not injected drugs into my arms. The rawhide strips represent how I was tied, gagged, tortured and left for dead. They also represent the bondage of these incessant memories."

The power of this imagery was overwhelming—horrific interpersonal experiences of a lifetime had been condensed into an inert object, literally becoming a totem of pain and loneliness. The clear boundaries around this revelation provided some degree of comfort that it would eventually end.

Sue continued, "Because this entity of trauma is all-encompassing and has frequently been a barrier to communication, trust, and love, I am asking my husband Tom to please come here and help me break this subjugation." Tom crossed the room to join his wife. She instructed him to stand behind her, toes touching her heels, and then with his arms reaching around her, to grab the ends of the stick. In this unique embrace, with tears streaming down her face, they paused, and then with a gasp the Sue and Tom simultaneously moved their hands to break the stick, which flew into many pieces. Letting go of the remaining pieces in their hands, they embraced each other. Her privately held burden had been transformed into a visceral body experience shared with her husband.

This visceral body experience was also shared by the audience, most of whom broke out into weeping as they witnessed both the revelation of trauma, and the bridging of the void as the couple joined together as one in breaking the stick. The juxtaposition of terror and intimacy, enacted symbolically here in the ceremony, seemed to speak more clearly than any words could have.

Roles within the Ceremony

The constituent roles within the ceremony represent different levels of society and provide opportunities for the disturbances at each level to be addressed. Throughout, the focus is less on the past than on the present and future.

The Leader

The group leader represents the authority in this temporary social structure, that is, the power that authorizes the ceremony. This authority derives from two sources: the truth and courage of the women's personal experience, and society's endorsement of the mental health professional's expertise. The leader therefore represents both the group members and society. This dual role provides the model for integrating the trauma survivor into normal society. It models for the client the capacity of being a trauma survivor and a member of society. In addition, because so often traumatic events occur as a result of the inattention, incompetence, corruption, or intention of the "authority," the leader's presence and actions serve as a model for how authorities in our society should act (Lubin & Johnson, 2000).

The leader's function is also to maintain the structure of the ceremony and the formality of the procedure, which are required for the containment of the aroused emotions and heightened anxieties. The leader's authority with group members will have been established through the course of the group sessions. In order to establish authority with the audience, the leader should be very active prior to the commencement of the ceremony, by introducing herself to each guest and reviewing with them personally what will happen during the ceremony. The leader should also use the time spent rehearsing the audience as an opportunity to establish her authority. As a person immersed in the awareness of trauma, yet functional in the world, the leader ultimately symbolizes the goal of the therapeutic enterprise, to move on in spite of the trauma, to bear a burden without denial.

The Witnesses

The witnesses are the invitees of the clients. They represent the client's social network and her current support system. During the ceremony, the witnesses stand and face the client across the room. The distance between the two symbolizes the distance they have to bridge in order to achieve a meaningful connection. It also highlights the importance of standing face to face in direct communication. No longer does the client have to avoid a meaningful exchange because it may reveal her secret. The encounter invites the witness into the inner world of the client where she has kept her traumatic memory concealed from everyone. The witnesses' affirmations and validations of the client's experience after her testimony empower the client's voice and effort in recovery. Often family members feel inadequate in their attempt to support the client due to the enormity of the trauma and its sequelae. Honoring the role of the witnesses in the healing process supports their efforts.

Survivors

The survivors are at the center of the ceremonial transformation: whether they will be able to withstand the forces against them, or withdraw again, becomes the subject of everyone's attention. By actively memorializing these meaningless acts of violence, by turning them into narratives of survival, the women attain recovery. Their acts of testimony place the trauma victims in the role of educators. They can now, if they choose, exercise control. They decide how to tell the story, whom to invite as witnesses, and how much to disclose. The energy that was invested in keeping the secret can be redirected toward the future and healing. Their ability to evoke emotions in the audience during the testimony demonstrates to the clients their affiliation with others in society. Sharing the burden with their support system and society reestablishes their connection to their family and community. In this way, the orientation of the ceremony is on the present and the future, not the past.

Audience

The ceremony occurs in a public setting to reestablish the commitment of society to its members. The audience represents society and therefore its active participation in the ceremony is crucial. During the ceremony the audience responds in unison. The loud response by the audience is a metaphor for the strength of its responsibility for and commitment to the recovery process. The loud voices of the audience shut out the voices of shame and blame. The presence of the audience/society also allows for a positive homecoming experience to occur. The audience's responses are the greeting the clients never received as they returned home from their war against the demons and ghosts of the trauma. Honoring such courage is the responsibility of society, as it is society that failed to protect them.

"Breaking the Silence Book"

During the years of conducting ceremonies we have collected many testimonies, poems, writings, and art works by the women and compiled them in the "Breaking the Silence Book," which is publicly displayed in our center. This book is available to people to learn about the aftermath of trauma. It functions as a documentation and memorialization of the traumatic experiences, illustrating the transcendence of traumatic events into courageous healing stories.

SPECIFIC PROCEDURES FOR CONDUCTING THE GRADUATION CEREMONY

Prior to the Ceremony

Even though each client is informed about the ceremony during the screening meeting, as the group progresses, resistance to the ceremony will mount. It is important that the therapist acknowledge the anxiety associated with such work and offers the reasons for its importance. The ceremony is an essential part of the treatment and each client is required to participate. If, despite the therapist's efforts to overcome the resistance, a group member comes to the ceremony without a witness, then the therapist should choose someone from the audience who will best represent the desired witness for this woman. It is useful to choose someone who can represent somebody of importance to her, such as a young woman to represent her estranged sister; an older man to represent a deceased father. The therapist or other group members should not be employed as witnesses, since the intent is for the witness to represent someone outside the "trauma circle," who is welcoming the survivor back into society.

During the Ceremony

Here is a list of the specific instructions.

1. Audience gathers in the ceremony room. Clarify who is going to function as a witness for each woman. A survivor may have more than one witness.
2. Survivors meet in another room.
3. Review with the audience how it will partake in the ceremony. Hand out the ceremony sheets to the audience. (These are not given to the graduating women.) Tell them that you will function as the Master of Ceremonies. The audience will repeat after you in unison each of the lines in bold print except for the

first one ("Are you willing to witness. . . . ."), to which every-one should respond directly.

4. Rehearse one or two of these lines with the audience.

5. Lead the women into the ceremony room. Your voice and de-meanor should be formal now. Ask them to form a line behind you, facing the audience.

6. Use recorded song/music of your choice to set the mood for the ceremony. It helps to transform the room into the ceremo-nial space.

7. Each woman is asked to say goodbye to her group members and to step forward by your side, one at a time.

8. Ask her witness(es) to stand up facing her on the other side of the room. It is important that there be distance between them.

9. Start the ceremony, following the ceremony sheet. If the woman begins to cry, simply place your hand on her shoulder and encourage her to continue. If she says something that does not fit with the expected response, do not indicate any neg-ativity. If family members interrupt out of concern for her, tell them that now is her time to speak. After the woman tells about her struggle and presents her testimony, ask her wit-nesses to tell her how they feel. Allow for spontaneous inter-action. If a nonverbal exchange occurs, such as an embrace, let it happen, but then ask the witness to verbalize his or her feelings. A direct verbal communication between the woman and her witness is an essential component of the therapeutic intervention.

10. After this exchange ask her to join her witnesses. This is a symbolic representation of the transformation. First they are apart and then she unites with her family and the audience (so-ciety).

11. This part of the ceremony is very emotional and evocative. Al-low time for everyone to experience it.

12. Repeat the ceremony for each of the women.

13. At the end of the ceremony, conclude by highlighting the im-portance of and the power of being part of the healing process.

"Today we have witnessed the courage of these women to face darkness and to fight the voices of despair. Trauma oc-curs alone—today we stand here together. Trauma silences the person—today their voices are loud and clear. Trauma is about hopelessness and despair—today we are filled with hope and pride. Today we win against the trauma. Thank you for being part of our healing."

14. Invite all participants to join for refreshments and informal social interaction.

PART III.
ENSURING SUCCESS
WITH TRAUMA-CENTERED
GROUP PSYCHOTHERAPY

Chapter 9

Therapist Competencies and Challenges

CRITICAL THERAPIST CHARACTERISTICS

Therapist characteristics play a major role in the TCGP model. The therapist not only must be a skilled facilitator, but also someone comfortable in confronting head-on the darkness of trauma. The fundamental competency required by TCGP is this capacity to calmly engage with traumatic material (Hegeman & Wohl, 2000; Pearlman & Saakvitne, 1995). Traumatized individuals are particularly astute in detecting even the slightest avoidant impulse in the therapist. In fact they expect it. The therapist must communicate an unquestioned commitment to be present with the client, particularly when the memories of the trauma or the perpetrator emerge (Knight, 1997). Demonstration of this commitment is accomplished in three ways, each of which is essential for the therapist to master.

First, the therapist attends to verbal and nonverbal cues that indicate reemergence of a traumatic theme or schema, and is the first one to note it. Second, the therapist must demonstrate tolerance of the traumatic material and calmness in handling it when it surfaces. Any attempt by the therapist to avoid direct confrontation with the trauma signals to the clients that he or she fears their traumatic material. This results in silencing the clients and will provoke numerous displacements and disruptions. Third, the therapist must feel comfortable with the different projections that are commonly encountered in trauma-centered work (Schermer, 2005). At any given time during a session the therapist may represent the perpetrator, the victim, the collaborator, or the bystander. These projections may shift rapidly as different group members engage in the discussion. The therapist who feels comfortable only in the role of the caregiver or rescuer will have

Trauma-Centered Group Psychotherapy for Women
© 2008 by The Haworth Press, Taylor & Francis Group. All rights reserved.
doi:10.1300/6097_09

difficulty in these groups. In addition to the different projections, the therapist must be able to shift among different formal roles during the course of the treatment, including educator, witness, mentor, and fellow human being.

SPECIFIC CHALLENGES FOR THE THERAPIST

This section describes three particularly common challenges that may arise during the course of treatment, and which may require special attention or interventions on the part of the therapist. All are, however, merely extensions of the fundamental challenge of trauma-centered work in general.

Avoidance

Most theories of PTSD identify avoidance as a primary defense against the distress associated with traumatic recollection, which prevents working through the trauma. In order to restore the normative process of integration, avoidance needs to be identified and confronted.

In the TCGP model avoidance is confronted during the first meeting of the group. Early disclosure of the traumatic events forces clients to confront the trauma rather than avoid it. Often group members feel relief "to get it over with" so early, which contributes to the low dropout rate in this model. Telling the story early in the group process in the context of a heterogeneous trauma population enhances group cohesion. The fact that others can hear one's story respectfully immediately deepens the sense of trust in the group.

Another form of avoidance is a displacement of discussion onto here-and-now issues or situations. Addressing this displacement directly with a reference to the trauma helps the women identify maladaptive ways of handling their trauma. A direct discussion about their traumas helps the women direct their feelings and thoughts to what is usually avoided. The therapist must actively engage in confronting these tendencies toward avoidance and withdrawal. For example, when a group member directs her angry feelings about not being protected by her mother during the abuse toward the therapist who did not attend to her at the moment, the therapist must directly address the displacement of the woman's anger from her mother to the therapist. The therapist needs to name the displacement and to trace the angry feelings to the traumatic experience. By identifying the displacement and directly addressing the underlying trauma-related emotions, the avoidance is confronted and a proper recollection can take place such as in Case 9.1.

Case 9.1: Jill

Jill is a forty-five-year-old single woman. She is currently fully employed but reports having many difficulties with coworkers. She lives by herself and has no social contacts. She was physically and emotionally abused by her mother who was neglectful of her responsibilities to her children. During the first phase of the program she disclosed to the group her difficulties growing up in poverty and being required to do many chores in the house due to her mother's numerous responsibilities. Her father left the family when Jill was very young. Jill did not disclose to the group the level of abuse by her mother. During each meeting Jill announced to the group how different her experience was, since she was not sexually abused. She felt her trauma was less than the others' and therefore she had little to talk about. She often focused on her experience in the group and felt others did not understand her or knew her. It became apparent that this strategy helped her avoid dealing with her trauma. The therapist asked Jill what it was like to be so invisible. Jill reiterated her wish to be connected to others and to become more socially involved. The therapist instructed her to ask the group members what she needed to do to help herself reach her goal, namely, to form connections with others. Jill immediately replied that the group members do not know her yet and therefore would not be able to give her any advice on the matter. The therapist then asked her what it was like to be invisible in her home during her childhood. Jill became more animated, saying "It was much better not to be seen, specifically when my mother had her rages."

THERAPIST: So being invisible was protective for you. It was your way to hide from your mother's rage.

JILL: (Nods and becomes visibly more anxious).

THERAPIST: I wonder if your attempt to stay invisible in our group protects you from the pain associated with your abuse?

JILL: (Tearful.) My mother got mad. At times she got so angry without any provocation, and then she would strike us. I protected my younger sisters so I got the brunt of it. She sometimes threw furniture at me. If I ran out of the house, she would lock the door and not let me in for hours; no food, no bathroom (crying).

THERAPIST: Jill, it made sense then to be invisible so your mother would not hurt you as much. But now it is safe. You do not need to hide. No one is going to strike you here. By being so isolated now you add to your pain and you are again all alone.

The group supported Jill and her courage to disclose to them her story and her pain. They told her that her story deserved to be heard and she deserved to be cared for. They indicated to her that for the first time they were getting to know her and they liked what they saw.

In this example Jill utilized avoidance in order to ward off the pain and fear associated with her abuse. She displaced her attention to matters that deflected attention away from her. Although she was craving connection to others, she was terrified and actively sabotaged any efforts for connection. By addressing her displacement and tracing her defense to the traumatic event, the therapist allowed Jill to experience her feelings in a controlled way, leading to the support and contact that she so desired.

Heightened Emotional Arousal

It is absolutely essential that the therapist be able to tolerate high levels of anxiety and heightened emotional arousal during group therapy. If for whatever reason the therapist finds herself attempting to avoid it or to deflect it, then she must address her discomfort with supervision. Heightened emotional arousal is not only a PTSD symptom but it is a human response to the encounter with the trauma. In some ways it is essential to evoke these authentic trauma-related feelings in order to introduce a meaningful change. In the TCGP model high emotional arousal detected in one of the group members signals to the therapist the possibility of the emergence of a traumatic schema. It calls for the attention of the therapist to identify traumatic themes or behaviors that are reenacted during the group process. The therapist's task is to look for verbal or nonverbal signs, such as emotional arousal, that may provide a window into the inner experience of the traumatized individual.

At times the theme of the minilecture may increase the emotional barometer of the group. Usually these topics tend to evoke shame or fear, such as the discussion about the woman's relationship to her body and her gender identity. Another example of heightened emotional arousal and vulnerability is the emergence of images of the perpetrator. It is very important that the therapist acknowledge them and state clearly what is occurring in the group. If the therapist misses it, ignores it, or avoids it, some group members will likely experience the therapist as the bystander or the perpetrator herself. Feelings of disappointment in the therapist who neglected to protect them and avoided an opportunity for reparation may be evoked. It is therefore very important for the therapist to be highly sensitive to heightened emotional arousal. The therapist must be prepared to identify these feelings, connect them to the client's trauma and response to trauma, and to provide the relevant concepts that illustrate how to deal with them. The information on the board from the minilecture is an effective way to introduce more adaptive ways of dealing with and processing these feelings. Making a reference to the board at these moments provides an intellectual framework for what is being experienced as purely visceral and gut-wrenching. The recognition of the perpetrator's presence in the group paradoxically relinquishes his power over the group members. Case 9.2 poignantly demonstrates the importance of this process.

Case 9.2: Karen

Karen survived a near-fatal truck accident. She is a truck driver and took pride in her job. After her accident and lengthy recuperation she developed PTSD and severe panic disorder which prevented her from resuming her job. Karen grew up in an environment that put women down and treated them as less capable. Karen decided to pursue a driving career in order to work in an exclusively male environment and to demonstrate to her family her worth as a woman. Karen did very well and made a nice living. She raised four children and is a committed mother. The car accident left her not only with physical and psychological wounds, but with a tremendous void and sense of disappointment. During the group she was a very active member, often offering support to others. She spoke openly about her accident and expressed her distress about not driving yet. She received support from the group who also encouraged her to take her time. She often came to the group with worn pants and dirty hands. Her masculine identity was apparent to all members of the group. When the therapist gave the lecture about "womanhood: your ally or your enemy?" Karen became very distressed. Her body tensed up and she became somewhat agitated, shaking her legs rapidly. The therapist noticed the abrupt change in Karen's level of arousal during the lecture. After the lecture, the therapist asked her if she viewed her womanhood as her enemy. She replied with visible anxiety, admitting for the first time that although the truck accident was not her fault, she attributed it to her womanhood, to being a woman. The therapist pointed out to her that her family always devalued her gender and it seems that she believed them. Karen immediately responded to the therapist that she became a truck driver to prove her family wrong. She was able to see how she sabotaged her efforts by believing her gender betrayed her. She received a lot of support from other group members who also reminded her of her devotion and competence as a mother. One group member pointed out to her that on the board, nurturing and maternal instincts were listed as allies, not enemies. The therapist asked Karen if she viewed herself as a competent mother. She replied in the affirmative. Karen made an attempt to embrace her womanhood and to reject the notion of her incompetence as a woman from her family. During the program Karen became more open about her pride as a woman. Her motivation to go back to driving became based on her feelings of competency, rather than a reactive desire to prove herself to her family.

Dissociation

Despite the fact that many group members do have dissociative symptoms or dissociative spectrum diagnoses, dissociation occurs infrequently. When it does occur it usually happens in the context of a traumatic reenactment or heightened emotional arousal (Hegeman & Wohl, 2000). When a member in the group dissociates, the therapist should acknowledge it to the group and make sure that everyone understands what dissociation is. If the therapist is unable to bring the dissociated member back into the group discussion, then she should assure the rest of the group that the client is okay and continue with the group process. As soon as the dissociated member is no longer dissociating, the therapist then acknowledges such to the group and lets her know what took place during the time she was "out." It is very important to support the defense while it is being utilized, however to confront it gently later by illustrating to her what she missed. The therapist should always make sure to ask the client about her experience, how she might want it handled in the future, and what was helpful for her this time. Addressing dissociation in the context of trauma treatment helps reduce the anxiety and discomfort associated with its encounter as demonstrated in Case 9.3.

Case 9.3: Ellen

After the minilecture on "cutting off people continues your isolation," group members actively discussed the pros and cons of being alone. Some members felt very strongly that isolation was keeping them safe and preventing them from another traumatic experience, while others argued for the benefits of reaching out to people and staying connected to a support network. Ellen, who had spent most of her adult life isolated and withdrawn from social contacts, began rocking back and forth in her chair, staring at the wall to her left. The therapist addressed Ellen by name two times without a response. The group became silent and tremendously anxious. The therapist calmly explained that it appeared that Ellen had dissociated. She explained that Ellen had "departed" temporarily as a way of managing her level of distress and that she would probably "rejoin" the group when she felt more comfortable. The therapist then asked the members of the group if they knew what dissociation was and if they had ever witnessed or experienced it. Some members denied any knowledge of or experience with dissociation. The therapist gave a brief overview of dissociation, its usefulness as a defense mechanism during trauma, and how it is triggered by reminders of the trauma. The therapist explained to the group that most likely the discussion had reminded Ellen of her own trauma. The therapist then checked in with the group on how anxious they felt and they reported a high level of anxiety, but felt better talking about it. The therapist acknowledged that witnessing someone dissociate is anxiety provoking, because it demonstrates how powerful the past trauma is in controlling someone. "But Ellen will take her time, and when she will come back, I will review our discussion with her, but for now I would like us to continue from where we left off." The group continued the discussion without any difficulties. About ten minutes later it became apparent that Ellen had rejoined the group. The therapist then asked Ellen what had happened. She said she didn't know. She had not heard the therapist calling her name. The therapist then reviewed with Ellen what had happened. When asked about what the group should do if this happens in the future, Ellen said that she felt most comfortable to be left alone and allowed to return at her own pace. The therapist then asked her if she was able to listen to the other members' experiences, and she agreed. Each group member gave Ellen warm and caring words of encouragement. She thanked the group and acknowledged feeling less anxious.

Chapter 10

Empirical Support for Trauma-Centered Group Psychotherapy

After a period of development and clinical trials, we completed an empirical study of five cohorts of TCGP, which was published in 1998 (Lubin, Loris, Burt, & Johnson, 1998). This chapter is a summary of these findings.

Since that study, a total of twenty-two groups have been led using this model at our center, and twelve groups have been led by other clinicians at other centers (a total of 272 clients). Overall, the results appear to be consistently positive. Of the clients at our center, 75 percent have reported significant improvement in their condition after the groups. Only 2 percent have dropped out, and to our knowledge only four clients have worsened since participating. Further empirical studies are being designed to compare the results of TCGP with other types of treatment, such as individual therapy alone, supportive non-trauma-centered group therapy, and medication trials.

SUMMARY OF THE STUDY

This study examined the effectiveness of a sixteen-week trauma-centered group therapy in reducing primary symptoms of posttraumatic stress disorder (PTSD) in five groups (N = 29) of multiply traumatized women diagnosed with chronic PTSD. Assessments were made at baseline, at one-month intervals during treatment, at termination, and at six-month follow-up, using self-report and structured interview measures of PTSD and psychiatric symptomatology. Subjects showed significant reductions in all three clusters of PTSD

Trauma-Centered Group Psychotherapy for Women
© 2008 by The Haworth Press, Taylor & Francis Group. All rights reserved.
doi:10.1300/6097_10

symptoms (i.e., reexperiencing, avoidance, and hyperarousal) and depressive symptoms, and near significant reductions in general psychiatric and dissociative symptoms, at termination. These improvements were sustained at six-month follow-up.

METHOD

Subjects

Female subjects were recruited from the community through advertisements and referrals from area agencies. Selection criteria included (1) ages eighteen to sixty-five; (2) victims or witnesses of violent crime, physical or sexual assault, or other emotionally traumatizing incidents in both childhood and adulthood (defined as serious threat to life or bodily integrity); and (3) willingness to participate in a group modality. Exclusion criteria included being in acute crisis, actively abusing substances, psychosis, current suicidality, or participation in another group therapy. Subjects were accepted on the condition that they made no changes in current treatment arrangements (i.e., individual therapy, medications, and twelve-Step programs). No fees were charged or payments made to subjects. Groups were formed with six to seven subjects.

For this study, fifty-six subjects were evaluated, and thirty-eight met inclusion criteria and were accepted into the study. Written informed consent was obtained from subjects after the purpose and procedures of the study were fully explained. Five subjects dropped out during the two- to three-week waiting period. Of thirty-three subjects entering the study, twenty-nine completed treatment. Four dropped out during phase one (one from each of the first four groups).

Therapists

Dr. Hadar Lubin served as the lead therapist for all five groups. Her co-leaders were a female clinical psychologist for four groups, and a female psychiatrist for one group, who were trained in the treatment model prior to initiation of the study. Adherence to the treatment model was monitored by the lead therapist in supervision sessions immediately following each group session. All therapists were blind to the quantitative assessment data collected by research assistants.

Measures

Four trained clinician interviewers administered the study measures to subjects at baseline, one-month intervals during treatment, termination, and six-month follow-up. Each subject was assessed by the same interviewer for all assessments. This evaluation included a detailed review of trauma history and an assessment of PTSD and general psychiatric symptomatology. Diagnoses were determined using the Structured Clinical Interview for DSM-III-R (SCID).

PTSD measures

The *Clinician Administered PTSD Scale* (CAPS) assesses the symptom frequency and intensity of the seventeen PTSD symptoms listed in DSM-III-R (Blake et al., 1995). Both current (i.e., past week) and lifetime PTSD are assessed. In addition to the assessments at entry, termination, and follow-up, the CAPS was also administered to subjects at one-month, two-month, and three-month time-points during the treatment course. *Mississippi Scale for Civilian PTSD* (MISS) is a thirty-nine-item self-report questionnaire, adapted from the *Mississippi Scale for Combat-Related PTSD* by the original authors (Keane, Caddell, & Taylor, 1988). *Impact of Events Scale* (IES) is a fifteen-item scale that consists of two subscales: *Cognitive Intrusion* and *Avoidance* (Horowitz, Wilner, & Alvarez, 1979).

Measures of Psychiatric Symptomatology

The *Symptom Checklist-90-Revised* (SCL-90-R) is a ninety-item Likert scale covering a broad spectrum of psychiatric symptoms (Derogatis, 1977). The *Beck Depression Inventory* (BDI) is a twenty-one-item self-report questionnaire, which has been widely used in empirical research on depression in rape victims (Beck et al., 1961). The *Dissociative Experiences Scale* (DES) is a twenty-eight-item self-report scale that measures dissociative symptoms and experiences (Bernstein & Putnam, 1986).

Data Analysis

The analytic strategy consisted of two parts: first, in examining changes in outcome measures from pre- to posttreatment; and second, between treatment and six-month follow-up. Repeated measures ANOVAs or *t*-tests were used to determine overall main effects of treatment on dependent variables as well as to examine effects of each independent variable (cohort, age, age of traumas, type of trauma, type of perpetrator, recency of trauma, education, or marital status). Median splits were used for noncategorical variables. Due to multiple comparisons, the *p* value was set at .01.

RESULTS

Demographic Characteristics

Demographic data revealed the sample to be at a mean age of forty-one years old, primarily Caucasian, relatively educated and partially employed. These subjects generally experienced several traumas from childhood through adulthood. Subjects experienced sexual assault or rape (83 percent), physical assault (59 percent), and/or violent accidents (31 percent). Perpetrators were usually family members (66 percent), and less often acquaintances (24 percent) or strangers (10 percent). On average, their last trauma was over ten years before. The sample has remained severely ill for an extended length of time. On average, each subject met criteria for three DSM-III-R diagnoses, including 66 percent anxiety disorder, 52 percent mood disorder, 34 percent borderline personality disorder, 14 percent somatoform disorder, and 79 percent disorders of extreme stress. About half had been hospitalized and/or had attempted suicide. Their average Global Assessment of Functioning was 55 (SD = 7.42). The women had been in outpatient psychotherapy for an average of 7.6 years (SD = 3.4) prior to entry into the study, and during the study 83 percent were in individual therapy and 79 percent were on psychotropic medication (17 percent antipsychotics, 62 percent antidepressants, 55 percent antianxiety). There were no significant differences among the five cohorts on any of the study variables.

Pre- to Posttreatment Effects

Table 10.1 lists the main results of the study. Subjects demonstrated significant reductions in their PTSD symptoms as measured by the clinician interview (CAPS) on all subscales and total symptomatology (twenty-six of twenty-nine subjects improved). These reductions were evident within the first month of treatment and continued to show improvement through termination. Clinically meaningful reductions in CAPS scores (over one standard deviation below pretreatment levels, about a 50 percent reduction) occurred for 38 percent of the sample. The self-report measures of PTSD (MISS and IES) showed less robust reductions. Subjects showed significant reductions in depressive symptoms and near-significant reductions for improvement in overall psychiatric (SCL-90) and dissociative (DES) symptoms. On repeated measures ANOVAs, no differences in outcome were found between subgroups differing in age, age at trauma, type of trauma, type of perpetrator, recency of trauma, education, or marital status.

Follow-up Assessment

Table 10.1 also presents the data for the twenty-two subjects who completed the follow-up evaluation six months after termination of treatment.

TABLE 10.1. Repeated Measures ANOVAs on Outcome Measures, Pre- and Posttreatment

Measures	Entry N = 33	Completion N = 29	6-Month Follow-up N = 22	ANOVA F (2,42)
CAPS				
Reexperiencing	1.54	1.00	.97	6.90***
Avoidance	1.62	1.05	1.13	6.99***
Hyperarousal	1.73	1.34	1.44	4.52**
Total	1.64	1.13	1.17	10.42***
Mississippi	112.82	105.18	107.00	2.53
IES-Total	34.91	30.82	30.36	1.83
DES	508.04	417.91	389.27	3.18*
Beck Depression	22.18	15.14	18.14	4.43**
SCL-90	116.09	91.96	94.73	1.93

*p < .05; **p < .01; ***p < .001.

The seven who did not complete the follow-up evaluation did not significantly differ from the remaining sample on any dependent measure at entry. Overall, the data indicate that subjects maintained their gains on the PTSD symptoms, and showed some return toward baseline in depression and psychiatric distress. Subjects showed significant reductions at follow-up, in comparison to entry, on CAPS total score, and all three CAPS subscales, and the DES. Half of the sample showed clinically meaningful reductions in CAPS scores (i.e., one standard deviation lower).

Course of Illness

The larger context of course of illness and the impact of treatment can be gleaned by comparing these data with the Lifetime CAPS, which presumably is a measure of subjects' PTSD at its worst (usually several years prior to treatment). Figure 10.1 illustrates this relation. In comparison to the condition of PTSD at its worst (Lifetime), subjects had shown some improvement by the time they entered the study (approximately 17 percent reduction overall). The sixteen-week group therapy program produced another 27 percent reduction in these symptoms, followed by a 3 percent increase at six months.

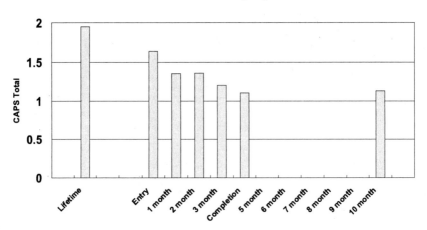

Figure 10.1.

DISCUSSION

This study, even with the six-month follow-up, is limited by the absence of a control or comparison group, so these results must be viewed as preliminary, since it is not possible to determine whether another type of treatment might have been as effective. Possible explanations other than treatment effect for the positive outcomes include (1) Hawthorne effect, (2) regression to the mean, (3) effects of concurrent individual and psychopharmacologic treatments, and (4) rater bias. However, the subjects in this sample had been suffering from stable levels of PTSD symptomatology despite multiple forms of treatment for many years prior to this study, and made no changes in their concurrent treatments during the study. Thus it is unlikely that they entered the study with high expectations, at especially difficult times, or in the midst of changes in their ongoing treatment regimens. Rater bias was addressed during training and every effort was made to minimize it through separation of treatment and assessment components. Raters had no knowledge of subjects' treatment experience.

The main results of this study show that this form of group therapy was consistently effective, across five cohorts of women, in reducing core PTSD symptoms, and secondarily in diminishing the levels of psychiatric distress. These gains were largely retained at six-month follow-up. The fact that gains were more prominent among PTSD symptoms than general psychiatric symptoms is strongly suggestive of a specific treatment effect. Improvement was stronger on the clinician-administered instrument, which probed for more details of symptoms, than the self-report measures, which had less specificity. Gains were equally evident among subjects varying in age, type and recency of trauma, type of perpetrator, education and marital status, suggesting that the treatment may have applicability to a wide range of trauma populations. These results are particularly encouraging given the severity of illness (e.g., extent of trauma, prior hospitalizations, high comorbidity), and treatment resistance (e.g., years of prior treatment) evident in this sample.

Chapter 11

Conclusion

We have found that group therapy can be a powerful means to help traumatized women achieve recovery from the wounds of the past. Sexual and physical abuse in childhood, rape, domestic violence, and other traumatic experiences are profoundly injurious, and their effects sink deeply into the soul. To look directly again at the event, to place the fear or terror in a new place, to open oneself to mourning, and to see clearly the wasted time and dashed hopes, which we have seen our clients do, is to show unimaginable courage. All of our efforts as health professionals should be directed toward giving our clients the strength to find this courage.

This book has described one form of group intervention for trauma and PTSD, Trauma-Centered Group Psychotherapy (TCGP), which we hope has provided you with a clear enough picture to be able to implement it in your setting with your clients. The method is based on a developmental perspective of trauma whose central concept of *differentiation* provides guidance in designing specific interventions. The method attempts to balance clients' needs for structure with the need to engage with the traumatic schemas sufficiently to allow transformation to occur. It should come as no surprise to anyone that many of the principles and techniques used in TCGP are similar to those used in other approaches, for our work has been deeply influenced by these other approaches. Though there are many roads to recovery, the general direction to health is being increasingly understood.

Readers may contact the authors for consultation on TCGP by writing us at: Post Traumatic Stress Center, 19 Edwards Street, New Haven, CT 06511, calling 203-624-2146, or e-mail: ptsdcenter@ sbcglobal.net.

Trauma-Centered Group Psychotherapy for Women
© 2008 by The Haworth Press, Taylor & Francis Group. All rights reserved.
doi:10.1300/6097_11

Appendix A

Handout for the Graduation Ceremony

The women, family members, friends, and guests gather. The leader enters the room followed by the group of women. In turn, each woman is asked to come forward, say goodbye to each of the other cohort members, and then stand next to the leader. Her family or friends are then asked to stand across the room from her, to be her witnesses. The audience, who have been given a copy of this ceremony, follow along, and when cued by the leader, speak loudly in unison.

LEADER: We come here today to break the silence and to listen to the untold. Are those gathered here willing to witness the stories of these women?

ALL: (in unison) Yes we are!

LEADER: Have you suffered a traumatic event as a child or as an adult? (woman answers) When you experienced your trauma did you feel terror, pain, or overwhelming fear? [woman answers]

ALL: That is trauma.

LEADER: As a result of the trauma, did you experience shame, guilt, and self-doubt? (woman answers)

ALL: You are not to blame.

LEADER: After the traumatic experience, were you put down, stigmatized, betrayed, or rejected? (woman answers)

ALL: You were let down!

LEADER: Did you feel confused, shut down, or isolated? (woman answers)

ALL: We are here tonight.

LEADER: As a result of your pain and the trauma did you cut off people that you love? (woman answers) Lose control of your anger and hurt people that you love? (woman answers)

Felt so numb that hurting yourself was the only thing to do? (woman answers)

Trauma-Centered Group Psychotherapy for Women
© 2008 by The Haworth Press, Taylor & Francis Group. All rights reserved.
doi:10.1300/6097_12

Did you resort to drugs or alcohol to silence the pain? (woman answers)

Did you think of suicide as a way of ending it all? (woman answers)

Is there still hope? (woman answers)

ALL: Yes we believe there is hope.

LEADER: Did you have experiences that kept you and your story silent? (woman answers)

ALL: We are listening now.

LEADER: Tell us about your struggle.

(Client then speaks or shows her creative project in her own way. After she is done, each family member or friend is then asked to speak to her from their hearts. After this, the woman crosses the room and joins her family. At the conclusion of the evening, everyone is asked to stay and socialize with refreshments.)

Appendix B

Workbooks

PHASE I WORKBOOK

Name:_____   Date:_____

The Journey from Shame to Empowerment

1. Disclosing the Trauma

2. Shame and Identity

3. The Void and Emptiness

4. Moving from Rage to Forgiveness

5. Womanhood: My Ally or My Enemy?

1. Disclosing the Trauma

Trauma is all about secrecy. By keeping your story silent you keep yourself hostage to the trauma. The perpetrator wants you to keep it secret so you continue to be vulnerable to perpetration and you get him or her off the hook. The trauma silenced your voice. Telling your story empowers you. Healing involves sharing the urden with others and freeing you from the hold of the trauma. Both are accomplished by telling your story. We are ready to listen. Start now.

_____

_____

_____

_____

_____

_____

_____

_____

_____

_____

_____

_____

_____

_____

2. Shame and Identity

Victims of trauma such as physical, sexual, or emotional abuse often believe they deserved the abuse. Because you were terrified when it occurred, out of this helplessness, you concluded, "I MUST BE BAD." For example: What is a child to believe if her own parent attacks or violates her? "Yes, I must be no good. I must have deserved it." So the shameful experience is internalized and becomes the way she views herself. Over the years, these internalized shameful experiences affect how a person feels, thinks, and behaves and, especially if these events occurred in childhood, the person's personality and identity can be dramatically affected.

1. Did you have experiences during childhood or adulthood that filled you with shame? What are these experiences?

_____

_____

_____

2. Do you find yourself avoiding situations that may remind you of these shameful experiences? What are those situations?

_____

_____

_____

3. What do you do to avoid these situations?

_____

_____

_____

4. What part of yourself do you feel ashamed about?

_____

_____

_____

3. The Void and Emptiness

When shameful and humiliating experiences become part of who you are, getting rid of them leaves you empty and scared. That is why many victims of trauma, especially early childhood trauma, feel an overwhelming sense of emptiness, almost like having a black hole inside. Thus looking inside often leaves you in the dark. If you had many traumatic experiences, then you are filled with a lot of these holes which may have developed into what is called a Personality Disorder, which can interfere with your self-esteem and relations with others. Many times there is a wish to fill up this hole, in order not to feel the void. Often traumatized individuals will attempt to fill the void with alcohol, drugs, food, and sex.

1. Do you ever look inside and find a big dark void?_____ What usually reminds you or causes you to experience this hole?

   _____

   _____

   _____

2. Do you find yourself running away from this feeling? In what way?

   _____

   _____

   _____

3. What do you do to attempt to fill up this overwhelming sense of emptiness?

   _____

   _____

   _____

4. What can you do instead of filling the void by self destructive means?

   _____

   _____

   _____

4. Moving from Rage to Forgiveness

There is no doubt that you have been shortchanged as a result of the way you were treated during your traumatic events. You deserve better than that, like any person who has been fortunate to have parents and friends who supported her and showed their love openly. You did not deserve to be abused, put down, humiliated, or neglected. But you were. When a person is shortchanged, particularly by someone who was supposed to love and protect them, they usually get filled up with rage and a wish for revenge. It is usually manifested by uncontrollable anger and rage attacks. That is understandable; the problem is that it leads to problems with relationships and eventually leads to isolation. If you can accept the fact that you were shortchanged and you are not to blame for the abuse, then you can forgive yourself. This forgiveness will allow you to move on, to be less bitter, and to be less angry.

1. Do you have problems with your anger or rage? How does it manifest itself?

_____

_____

2. What triggers your outbursts?

_____

_____

3. In what ways were you shortchanged?

_____

_____

4. In what ways can you show self-forgiveness?

_____

_____

5. Womanhood: My Ally or My Enemy?

Women who have been traumatized often have a conflicted relationship with their body and their gender. For some it affects their intimacy, for others it is a source of embarrassment and confusion. They may associate their womanhood with the pain from the abuse. Qualities such as weakness, vulnerability, submissiveness, and dependency become connected to being a woman, and being a victim. The result can be avoiding intimate relationships, avoiding sexuality, and avoiding parenthood. It is important to remember that being a woman did NOT cause your abuse; your perpetrator caused your abuse, out of a desire for power over you.

1. Are you challenged by your womanhood? How?

_____

_____

_____

2. In what ways do you treat your womanhood as an enemy?

_____

_____

_____

3. In what ways have you found to keep your womanhood as your ally?

_____

_____

_____

4. How might you change your behavior to embrace your womanhood more fully?

_____

_____

_____

PHASE II WORKBOOK

Name:_____   Date:_____

The Journey from Trauma to Recovery

1. You Are Not the Trauma

2. Knowing Your Symptoms Increases Your Control

3. Your Body Is Not Your Enemy

4. Cutting Off People Continues Your Isolation

5. Stop the Dumping

6. Putting It Right

1. You Are Not the Trauma

Trauma overwhelms the person's capacity to cope. You did whatever you needed to do in order to survive. It is not surprising that you built a thick wall to protect yourself from any possibility of harm. The problem is that when there is no danger, the walls you built around you interfere with your capacity to live your life. You became imprisoned by your own defenses.

1. In what ways has the trauma affected you as a person?

_____

_____

_____

_____

2. What are the walls that you put up to protect yourself?

_____

_____

_____

_____

3. How do your walls interfere with your life today?

_____

_____

_____

_____

4. What do you need to do in order to take down the walls?

_____

_____

_____

2. Knowing Your Symptoms Increases Your Control

The symptoms that you developed as a result of your trauma require constant attention and management. They also remind you of the trauma and therefore leave you terrified of them. Often traumatized individuals run scared from their symptoms, which usually leads to more symptoms. Knowing your symptoms and their triggers puts you in control and as a result you can become less symptomatic.

1. List the most disturbing symptoms that you have:

_____

_____

_____

2. What are the ways that you are running scared from your symptoms?

_____

_____

_____

_____

3. What triggers your depression, anger, isolation, or withdrawal?

_____

_____

_____

_____

4. What can you do to better manage your symptoms?

_____

_____

_____

_____

3. Your Body Is Not Your Enemy

During the abuse your body reacted with tension, fear, anxiety, disconnection, and pain. If the abuse was sexual then your body may have responded to the stimulation and left you confused and ashamed. These are all natural responses to trauma: your body focused on survival. It is not surprising that you treat your body as the enemy. Your body responded to the abuse; your body is not the perpetrator.

1. What does your body feel like when you get anxious?

_____

_____

2. In what ways do you treat your body as your enemy?

_____

_____

3. List the medical problems you have had since your traumatic event:

_____

_____

4. What problems do you have tolerating emotional or sexual intimacy?

_____

_____

5. Do you feel guilty about these things? How?

_____

_____

6. What do you do for exercise, diet, relaxation, or leisure?

_____

_____

4. Cutting off People Continues Your Isolation

In order to survive the trauma you had to cut off nearly everything and everybody. Some traumatized individuals need to cut off parts of themselves in order to survive it. We call this dissociation. These defense mechanisms are essential in the pursuit of survival. However, when there is no longer any danger, they interfere with living in the present. By cutting people off in your life now, you continue to be as isolated as you felt during the trauma.

1. Who among your family or friends have you cut off?

_____

_____

2. Who would you like to be able to communicate with again?

_____

_____

3. Do you feel other people can not understand you?

_____

_____

4. How often do you break up relationships? What usually leads to it?

_____

_____

5. Have you found anyone who did not have your experience but still understood you?

_____

_____

5. Stop the Dumping

**Many people dumped on you during the trauma/abuse: the perpe-
trators, the bystanders, the community, and society. People blamed you
for being too quiet or too aggressive, too withdrawn or too hyperactive,
too tired or too vigilant, and on and on and on. Sound familiar? It is not
surprising you dump on others as a result of the way you were treated.
The people you most likely dump on are those that you love. The problem, though, is that they, like you, don't like to be dumped on and therefore dump on you in return. A vicious cycle is fueling your sense of isolation and disconnection. You need to break the cycle in order to build
connections that help you heal the scars of the trauma.**

1. How were you dumped on during and after your trauma?

_____

_____

2. Who in your life have you dumped on?

_____

_____

3. How have people in your life responded to your dumping?

_____

_____

4. What usually triggers your dumping?

_____

_____

5. What can you do to stop the dumping?

_____

_____

6. Putting It Right

It makes sense that when something terribly wrong happens to a person there will be an attempt to make the wrong right. It is a natural human response to try to get justice. In fact many times the people who should have protected you, (parents, caregiver, or family members), did not, could not, or would not. You were wronged and justice did not prevail. You were left with a heightened sensitivity to injustice and unfairness. Since you were not able to get justice during your trauma, you attempt to get justice whenever you detect injustice, which often leads to trouble. We call it displacement. That is why people who were traumatized have difficulty with dishonest or incompetent authority figures, and many times become litigious, in order to "put it right." While this may sometimes be a good thing in itself, you may find yourself undermining your efforts because your anger is too great, your intolerance too intense, for the current situation. The problem is that the original source of your pain, the original wrong that you suffered, is not corrected by it.

1. Do you find it intolerable when someone makes a mistake or does something wrong? Can you give examples?

_____

_____

_____

2. Do you find yourself preoccupied by thinking how to prove someone wrong or actually feel compelled to pursue it through legal channels?

_____

_____

_____

3. Can you think of examples of how you have displaced your wish to put right the wrong that was done to you?

_____

_____

_____

PHASE III WORKBOOK

Name:_____   Date:_____

The Journey from Isolation to Connection

1. Finding Meaning in Your Life

2. Moving into the Future

3. Saying Goodbye

4. Achieving Transformation

5. Standing in the Truth of One's Testimony

1. Finding Meaning in Your Life

Trauma is meaningless. It depletes the person's sense of welfare, worth, and purpose. The process of healing can generate meaning and therefore can contribute to the person's esteem, hope, and aspiration. In order to find meaning in your life you need to let people know of your ordeal, help others who are suffering, and find support.

1. Have you harbored resentment toward your family, other people, and society for not supporting you after your trauma?

_____

_____

_____

2. Do you think you can try to help other people who have suffered? How?

_____

_____

_____

3. How can you turn the rest of your life into something positive and meaningful by being a woman, by telling your story, and by actively trying to influence the world?

_____

_____

_____

4. List the ways that you can contribute to yourself, your family, and society as a woman:

_____

_____

_____

2. Moving into the Future

The voices of trauma are strong. They are trying to take control and keep you in the past. Often trauma victims feel that their own voice is silent. The voices of despair, hopelessness, shame, and demoralization are the voices of the trauma. In order to move on into the future, your voice needs to be heard. You have to tell people in your life about your ordeal; you have to educate people about the aftermath of the trauma. Are you ready to move on? Are you ready to speak up?

1. What are the voices of your trauma that continue to affect your life today?

_____

_____

_____

2. What do you usually do when the voices of the trauma take control?

_____

_____

_____

3. What brings them on?

_____

_____

_____

4. What can you do in order to gain control over the voices of the trauma?

_____

_____

_____

5. What can you do to make your voice stronger?

_____

_____

_____

3. Saying Goodbye

Trauma is all about loss. It is human nature to grieve after a loss. Since trauma is isolating, alienating, terrifying, and leaves the victim silent, the grief process does not occur. It is important to be able to mourn a loss in order to restore order in one's life. Traumatized individuals need to practice how to mourn in order to make room for life.

1. What are the losses you recognize as a result of your trauma?

_____

_____

_____

2. What do you do when you are faced with a metaphor of loss such as saying goodbye?

_____

_____

_____

3. In what ways does your trauma interfere with your capacity to grieve?

_____

_____

_____

4. In what ways can you practice saying goodbye?

_____

_____

_____

4. Achieving Transformation

Trauma causes destruction and fragmentation. Healing involves building new foundations and rehearsing many transformations. Although trauma occurs in isolation, the healing process requires social connection. These transformations occur every time you win against the forces of trauma.

1. What are the transformations that you have already achieved?

_____

_____

_____

2. What transformations are you hoping to make in the future?

_____

_____

_____

_____

3. Who in your life can help you to achieve these transformations?

_____

_____

_____

_____

4. What can you do in order to help other trauma victims?

_____

_____

_____

_____

5. Standing in the Truth of One's Testimony

The power of healing depends on your capacity to tell your story, teach others about the consequences of abuse, and take an active role in helping other trauma victims. By sharing your story you lighten your burden, let other people support you, and inspire other victims to engage in the process of healing.

1. What are different ways you can tell your story?

\
\
\

2. Who in your life can be a witness to your healing?

\
\
\

3. How has the group experience helped you heal?

\
\
\

4. What would you like people to know about your journey?

\
\
\

5. What life experiences have inspired your healing?

\
\
\

Appendix C

Women's Trauma Program

TREATMENT CONTRACT

Name:_____ Date:_____

   Welcome to the program. We are very happy you decided to participate in the program and we are honored to take part in your healing journey. Before commencing your participation we would like to review several rules and expectations that will assure that your treatment is conducted in a safe environment and that you will reap the benefits of the program.

1. I agree to attend all sessions of the program. In the event that I am not able to attend, I will call the Center beforehand to notify the group leader of my absence.
2. I understand that substance abuse of any kind will preclude my participation in the program and I agree not to come to the group under the influence of drugs or alcohol.
3. I agree to use appropriate language when I express anger and to refrain from any violent language or acts. If I do so, I understand that my continued participation will be reassessed and possibly terminated.
4. I understand that social contact with group members between sessions is permitted. However, I agree that I will only discuss other group members in their presence.
5. If I become aware of self-destructive behavior or suicidal thoughts by other group members outside of the group meeting, I will immediately inform the group leaders. I also understand that if I will share similar thoughts with a group member, she will be expected to inform the group leaders.
6. I am aware that I am expected to participate in the Graduation Ceremony at the end of the program.

I have read the above information and I agree to follow these rules.

_____   _____   _____
Client   Therapist   Co-therapist

Trauma-Centered Group Psychotherapy for Women
© 2008 by The Haworth Press, Taylor & Francis Group. All rights reserved.
doi:10.1300/6097_14

References

Abbott, B. (1995). Group therapy. In C. Classen (Ed.), *Treating women molested in childhood*. (pp. 95-127). San Francisco: Jossey-Bass.

Alexander, P., Neimeyer, R., Follete, V., Moore, M., & Harter, S. (1989). A comparison of group therapy treatment of women sexually abused as children. *Journal of Consulting and Clinical Psychology, 57*(4), 479-483.

American Psychiatric Association. (1994). *Diagnostic and statistical manual of mental disorders* (Fourth Edition-Revised.). Washington, DC: American Psychiatric Association.

Beck, A., & Emery, G. (1985). *Anxiety disorders and phobias*. New York: Basic Books.

Beck, A., Ward, C., Mendelsohn, M., Mock, J., & Erbaugh, J. (1961). An inventory for measuring depression. *Archives of General Psychiatry, 4*, 561-571.

Bernstein, E.M. & Putnam, F.W. (1986). Development, reliability, and validity of a dissociation scale. *Journal of Nervous Mental Disease, 174*, 727-735.

Blake, D.D., Weathers, R., Nagy, L.M., Kaloupek, D.G., Klauminzer, G., Charney, D.C., et al. (1995). The development of a clinician-administered PTSD scale. *Journal of Traumatic Stress, 8*, 75-90.

Bloch, D.A. (1987). Family, disease, treatment systems: A coevolutionary model. *Family Systems Medicine, 5*, 277-292.

Bloom, S. (1997). *Creating sanctuary*. New York: Routledge.

Brende, J. (1983). The psychodynamic view of character pathology in Vietnam combat veterans. *Bulletin of the Menninger Clinic, 47*, 193-216.

Briere, J. (1992). *Child abuse trauma: Theory and treatment of the lasting effects*. Newbury Park, CA: Sage.

Bruner, J. (1964). The course of cognitive growth. *American Psychologist, 19*, 1-6.

Catherall, D. (1989). Differentiating intervention strategies for primary and secondary trauma in post-traumatic stress disorder: The example of Vietnam veterans. *Journal of Traumatic Stress, 2*, 289-304.

Chard, K. (2005). An evaluation of cognitive processing therapy for the treatment of posttraumatic stress disorder related to childhood sexual abuse. *Journal of Consulting and Clinical Psychology, 73*, 965-971.

Classen, C., Koopman, C., Nevill-Manning, K., & Spiegel, D. (2001). A preliminary report comparing trauma-focused and present-focused group therapy against a wait-listed condition among childhood sexual abuse survivors with PTSD. *Journal of Aggression, Maltreatment, and Trauma, 4,* 265-288.

Cloitre, M., & Koenen, K. (2001). The impact of borderline personality disorder on process group outcome among women with posttraumatic stress disorder related to childhood abuse. *International Journal of Group Psychotherapy, 51,* 379-398.

Cole, C., & Barney, E. (1987). Safeguards and the therapeutic window: A group treatment strategy for adult incest survivors. *American Journal of Orthopsychiatry, 57,* 601-609.

Courtois, C.A. (1988). *Healing the incest wound.* New York: Norton.

Derogatis, L.R. (1977). *SCL-90: Administration. Scoring and procedure manual-1.for the revised version.* Baltimore: John Hopkins University School of Medicine.

Fallot, R., & Harris, M. (2002). The trauma recovery and empowerment model (TREM): Conceptual and practical issues in a group intervention for women. *Community Mental Health Journal, 38,* 475-485.

Figley, C. (1985). *Trauma and its wake: The study and treatment of post-traumatic stress disorder.* New York: Brunner/Mazel.

Foa, E.B., & Kozak, M.J. (1986). The emotional processing of fear: Exposure to corrective information. *Psychological Bulletin, 99,* 20-35.

Foa, E.B., Rothbaum, O.B., Riggs, D.S., & Murdock, T.B. (1991). Treatment of post-traumatic stress disorder in rape victims: A comparison between cognitive-behavioral procedure and counseling. *Journal of Consulting and Clinical Psychology, 59,* 715-723.

Foy, D., Glynn, S., Schnurr, P., Jankowski, M., Wattenberg, M., Weiss, D., et al. (2000). Group therapy. In E. Foa, T. Keane, & M. Friedman (Eds.), *Effective treatments for PTSD* (pp. 155-175). New York: Guilford.

Foy, D., Ruzek, J., Glynn, S., Riney, S., & Gusman, F. (2002). Trauma focus group therapy for combat-related PTSD: An update. *Journal of Clinical Psychology, 58,* 907-918.

Foy, D., Schnurr, P., Weiss, D., Wattenberg, M., Glynn, S., Marmar, C., et al. (2001). Group psychotherapy for PTSD. In J. Wilson, M. Friedman, & J. Lindy (Eds.), *Treating psychological trauma and PTSD* (pp. 183-202). New York: Guilford.

Glodich, A., & Allen, J. (1998). Adolescents exposed to violence and abuse: A review of the group therapy literature with an emphasis on preventing traumatic reenactment. *Journal of Child and Adolescent Group Therapy, 8,* 135-154.

Goodman, B., & Nowak-Scibelli, D. (1985). Group treatment for women incestuously abused as children. *International Journal of Group Psychotherapy, 35,* 531-544.

Green, B., Wilson, J., & Lindy, J. (1985). Conceptualizing post-traumatic stress disorder: A psychosocial framework. In C. Figley (Ed.), *Trauma and its wake: The study and treatment of post-traumatic stress disorder* (pp. 53-69). New York: Brunner/Mazel.

Harris, M. (1998). *Trauma recovery and empowerment.* New York: Free Press.

Hazzard, A., Rogers, J.H., & Angert, L. (1993). Factors affecting group therapy outcome for adult sexual abuse survivors. *International Journal of Group Psychotherapy, 43,* 453-468.

Hegeman, E., & Wohl, A. (2000). Management of trauma-related affect, defenses, and dissociative states. In R. Klein & V. Schermer (Eds.), *Group psychotherapy for psychological trauma* (pp. 64-88). New York: Guilford.

Herman, J. (1992a). Complex PTSD: A syndrome in survivors of prolonged and repeated trauma. *Journal of Traumatic Stress, 5,* 377-391.

Herman, J. (1992b). *Trauma and recovery.* New York: Basic Books.

Herman, J., & Schatzow, E. (1984). Time limited group therapy for women with history of incest. *International Journal of Group Psychotherapy, 34,* 605-616.

Horowitz, M. (1976). *Stress response syndromes.* New York: Jason Aronson.

Horowitz, M., Wilner, N., & Alvarez, W. (1979). Impact of events scale: A measure of subjective stress. *Psychosomatic Medicine, 41,* 209-218.

Jacobson, E. (1964). *The self and object world.* New York: International Universities Press.

Janoff-Bulman, R. (1992). *Shattered assumptions.* New York: MacMillan.

Johnson, D. (1987). Therapeutic rituals in the nursing home. In S. Sandel, & D. Johnson, *Waiting at the gate: Creativity and hope in the nursing home,* (pp. 151-172). Binghamton, NY: The Haworth Press.

Johnson, D., Feldman, S., Southwick, S., & Charney, D. (1994). The concept of the second generation program in the treatment of post-traumatic stress disorder among Vietnam veterans. *Journal of Traumatic Stress, 7,* 217-236.

Johnson, D., Feldman, S., Lubin, H., & Southwick, S. (1995). The use of ritual and ceremony in the treatment of post-traumatic stress disorder. *Journal of Traumatic Stress, 8,* 283-299.

Johnson, D., & Lubin, H. (2000). Group therapy for the symptoms of posttraumatic stress disorder. In R. Klein & V. Schermer (Eds.), *The healing circle: Group psychotherapy for psychological trauma,* (pp. 141-169). New York: Guilford.

Johnson, D., Lubin, H., Rosenheck, R., Fontana, A., Southwick, S., & Charney, D. (1997). Measuring the impact of homecoming on the development of post-traumatic stress disorder: The West Haven Homecoming Stress Scale. *Journal of Traumatic Stress, 10,* 259-278.

Keane, T.M., Caddell, J.M., & Taylor, K. (1988). Mississippi scale for combat-related PTSD. *Journal of Consulting and Clinical Psychology, 56,* 85-90.

Klein, R., & Schermer, V. (2000). *Group psychotherapy for psychological trauma.* New York: Guilford.

Knight, C. (1997). Critical roles and responsibilities of the leader in a therapy group for adult survivors of child sexual abuse. *Journal of Child Sexual Abuse, 6,* 21-37.

Kohut, H. (1977). *The restoration of the self.* New York: International Universities Press.

Krystal, H. (1988). *Integration and self-healing: Affect, trauma, alexithymia.* Hillsdale, NJ: Lawrence Erlbaum/Analytic Press.

Lane, R., & Schwartz, G. (1987). Levels of emotional awareness: A cognitive-developmental theory and its application to psychopathology. *American Journal of Psychiatry, 144,* 133-143.

Lifton, R. (1988). Understanding the traumatized self: Imagery, symbolization, and transformation. In J. Wilson, Z. Harel, & B. Kahana (Eds.), *Human adaptation to extreme stress,* (pp. 7-31). New York: Plenum Press.

Linehan, M. (1993). *Cognitive-behavioral treatment of borderline personality disorder.* New York: Guilford.

Lubin, H., & Johnson, D. (1997). Interactive psychoeducational group therapy for traumatized women. *International Journal of Group Psychotherapy, 47,* 271-290.

Lubin, H., & Johnson, D. (1998). Healing ceremonies. *Family Therapy Networker, 22,* 39-42.

Lubin, H., & Johnson, D. (2000). Psychoeducational group therapy in the treatment of authority problems in combat-related posttraumatic stress disorder. *International Journal of Group Psychotherapy, 50,* 277-296.

Lubin, H., & Johnson, D. (2003). The use of ceremony in multiple family therapy for psychological trauma. In D. Wiener & L. Oxford, (Eds.), *Action therapy with families and groups* (pp. 75-102). Washington, DC: American Psychological Association Books.

Lubin, H., Johnson, D., & Southwick, S. (1996). Impact of childhood abuse on adult psychopathology: A case report. *Dissociation, 9,* 134-139.

Lubin, H., Loris, M.., Burt, J., & Johnson, D. (1998). Efficacy of psychoeducational group therapy in reducing symptoms of posttraumatic stress disorder among multiply-traumatized women. *American Journal of Psychiatry, 155,* 1172-1177.

Lundqvist, G., & Ojehagen, A. (2001). Childhood sexual abuse: An evaluation of a two-year group therapy in adult women. *European Psychiatry, 16,* 64-67.

McCann, I.L., & Pearlman, L.A. (1990). *Psychological trauma and the adult survivor.* New York: Brunner/Mazel.

Mahler, M., Pine, R, & Bergman, A. (1975). *The psychological birth of the human infant.* New York: Basic Books.

Margolin, J. (1999). *Breaking the silence: Group therapy for childhood sexual abuse.* Binghamton, NY: The Haworth Press.

Marmar, C. R., Foy, D., Kagan, B., & Pynoos, R. (1993). An integrated approach for treating post-traumatic stress. In J.M. Oldham, M.B. Riba, & A. Tasman (Eds.), *American Psychiatric Association Review of Psychiatry, Vol. 12* (pp. 239-272). Washington, DC: American Psychiatric Press.

Meyer, P. (2000). Variety is the spice: Survivor groups of mixed sexual orientation. *Journal of Gay and Lesbian Social Services, 12,* 91-106.

Morgan, T., & Cummings, A. (1999). Change experienced during group therapy by female survivors of childhood sexual abuse. *Journal of Consulting and Clinical Psychology, 67,* 28-36.

Najavits, L., Weiss, R., Shaw, S., & Muenz, L. (1998). "Seeking safety:" Outcome of a new cognitive-behavioral psychotherapy for women with posttraumatic stress disorder and substance dependence. *Journal of Traumatic Stress, 11*, 437-456.

Neimeyer, R., Harter, S., & Alexander, P. (1991). Group perceptions as predictors of outcome in the treatment of incest survivors. *Psychology Research, 1*, 148-158.

Nicholas, M., & Forrester, A. (1999). Advantages of heterogeneous therapy groups in the psychotherapy of the traumatically abused: Treating the problem as well as the person. *International Journal of Group Psychotherapy, 49*, 323-342.

Parson, E. R. (1985). Post-traumatic accelerated cohesion: Its recognition and management in group treatment of Vietnam veterans. *Group, 9*, 10-23.

Pearlman, L. & Saakvitne, K. (1995). Cotherapists' countertransference in group therapy with incest survivors. In L. Pearlman & K. Saakvitne, *Trauma and the therapist*, (pp. 232-254). New York: Norton.

Pelcovitz, D., van der Kolk, B., Roth, S., Mandel, E, Kaplan, S., & Resick, P. (1997). Development of a criteria set and a structured interview for disorders of extreme stress. *Journal of Traumatic Stress, 10*, 3-16.

Piaget, J. (1962). *Play, dreams, and imitation in childhood.* New York: Norton.

Putnam, R. (1989). *Diagnosis and treatment of multiple personality disorder.* New York: Guilford.

Resick, P. & Schnicke, M. (1993). *Cognitive processing therapy for rape victims.* Newbury Park, CA: Sage.

Roth, S., Dye, E., & Lebowitz, L. (1988). Group therapy for sexual assault victims. *Psychotherapy, 25*, 82-93.

Roth, S., Newman, E., Pelcovitz, D., van der Kolk, B., & Mandel, R. (1997). Complex PTSD in victims exposed to sexual and physical abuse. *Journal of Traumatic Stress, 10*, 539-556.

Ryan, M., Nitsun, M., Gilbert, L., & Mason, H. (2005). A prospective study of the effectiveness of group and individual psychotherapy for women CSA survivors. *Psychology and Psychotherapy: Theory, Research, and Practice, 78*, 465-479.

Saxe, B., & Johnson, S. (1999). An empirical investigation of group treatment for a clinical population of adult female incest survivors. *Journal of Child Sexual Abuse, 8*, 67-88.

Schermer, V. (2005). Introduction to "Group therapist countertransference to trauma and traumatogenic situations." *International Journal of Group Psychotherapy, 55*, 1-29.

Schnurr, P., Friedman, M., Foy, D., Shea, T., Hsieh, F., Lavori, P., et al. (2003). Randomized trial of trauma-focused group therapy for posttraumatic stress disorder. *Archives of General Psychiatry, 60*, 481-489.

Schultz, R. (1990). Secrets of adolescence: Incest and developmental fixations. In R.P. Kluft (Ed.), *Incest-related syndromes of adult psychopathology* (pp. 133-160). Washington, DC: American Psychiatric Press.

Scurfield, R.M. (1993). Treatment of post-traumatic stress disorder among Vietnam veterans. In J.P. Wilson & B. Raphael, (Eds.), *International handbook of traumatic stress syndromes* (pp. 879-888). New York: Plenum Press.

Silver, S., & Wilson, J. (1988). Native American healing and purification rituals for war stress. In Wilson, J., Harel, Z., and Kahana, B. (Eds.), *Human adaptation to extreme stress,* (pp. 337-356). New York: Plenum Press.

Spiegel, D., Classen, C., Thurston, E., & Butler, L. (2004). Trauma-focused versus present-focused models of group therapy for women sexually abused in childhood. In L. Koenig, L. Doll, A. O'Leary, & W. Pequegnat (Eds.), *From child sexual abuse to adult sexual risk: Trauma, revictimization, and intervention,* (pp. 251-268). Washington, DC: American Psychological Association.

Titchener, J. (1986). Post-traumatic decline: A consequence of unresolved destructive drives. In C. Figley (Ed.), *Trauma and its wake. Vol. II* (pp. 5-19). New York: Brunner/Mazel.

Touigny, M., Hebert, M., Daigneault, I., & Simoneau, A. (2005). Efficacy of a group therapy for sexually abused adolescent girls. *Journal of Child Sexual Abuse, 14,* 71-93.

van der Kolk, B. (1987). The role of the group in the origin and resolution of the trauma response. In B. van der Kolk, (Ed.), *Psychological trauma* (pp. 153-171). Washington, DC: American Psychiatric Association Press.

van der Kolk, B. (2005). Developmental trauma disorder. *Psychiatric Annals, 35,* 401-408.

VanDeusen, K., & Carr, J. (2003). Recovery from sexual assault: An innovative two-stage group therapy model. *International Journal of Group Psychotherapy, 53,* 201-224.

Wallis, D. (2002). Reduction of trauma symptoms following group therapy. *Australian and New Zealand Journal of Psychiatry, 36,* 67-74.

Werner, H. (1948). *The comparative psychology of mental development.* New York: Science Editions.

Werner, H. & Kaplan, S. (1963). *Symbol formation.* New York: Wiley.

Winnicott, D. (1953). Transitional objects and transitional phenomena. In *Collected Papers* (pp. 229-242). New York: Basic Books.

Wolfsdorf, B., & Zlotnick, C. (2001). Affect management in group therapy for women with posttraumatic stress disorder and histories of childhood sexual abuse. *Journal of Clinical Psychology, 57,* 169-181.

Yalom, I. (1976). *The theory and practice of group psychotherapy.* New York: Basic Books.

Zlotnick, C., Shea, T., Rosen, K., Simpson, E., Mulrenin, K., Begin, A., et al. (1997). An affect-management group for women with posttraumatic stress disorder and histories of childhood sexual abuse. *Journal of Traumatic Stress, 10,* 425-436.

Index

('i' indicates an illustration; 't' indicates a table)

Trauma-Centered Group Psychotherapy for Women
© 2008 by The Haworth Press, Taylor & Francis Group. All rights reserved.
doi:10.1300/6097_16   *153*